W9-BVG-915

directions

new   FOR
STUDENT
SERVICES

number 5   •   1979

new directions for student services

a quarterly sourcebook
Ursula Delworth and Gary R. Hanson, Editors-in-Chief

number 5, 1979

consulting
on campus

Theodore Lownik Library
Illinois Benedictine College
Lisle, Illinois 60532

m. kathryn hamilton
charles j. meade
guest editors

Jossey-Bass Inc., Publishers
San Francisco • Washington • London

LB
2363
. C663

CONSULTING ON CAMPUS
New Directions for Student Services
Number 5, 1979
    M. Kathryn Hamilton, Charles J. Meade, Guest Editors

Copyright © 1979 by Jossey-Bass Inc., Publishers
and
Jossey-Bass Limited

Copyright under International, Pan American, and Universal
Copyright Conventions. All rights reserved. No part of
this issue may be reproduced in any form — except for brief
quotation (not to exceed 500 words) in a review or professional
work — without permission in writing from the publishers.

New Directions for Student Services is published quarterly
by Jossey-Bass Inc., Publishers. Subscriptions are available
at the regular rate for institutions, libraries, and agencies
of $25 for one year. Individuals may subscribe at the special
professional rate of $15 for one year. Application to mail at
second-class postage rates is pending at San Francisco, California,
and at additional mailing offices.

Correspondence:
Subscriptions, single-issue orders, change of address notices,
undelivered copies, and other correspondence should be sent to
New Directions Subscriptions, Jossey-Bass Inc., Publishers,
433 California Street, San Francisco, California 94104.
Editorial correspondence should be sent to the Editors-in-Chief,
Ursula Delworth, University Counseling Service, Iowa
Memorial Union, University of Iowa, Iowa City, Iowa 52242
or Gary R. Hanson, Office of the Dean of Students,
Student Services Building, Room 101, University of Texas
at Austin, Austin, Texas 78712.

Library of Congress Catalogue Card Number LC 78-73937

Cover design by Willi Baum

Manufactured in the United States of America

contents

editors' notes

The essence of campus consultation is in defining, understanding, and using knowledge of a complex system—the university community—to improve that system. Student services professionals engage in consultation daily; many believe, as we do, that consultation is the backbone of effective service to students. Yet very few professionals have had formal training in it; our professional literature scarcely acknowledges consultation on campus. Its evaluation lags far behind that of more direct, traditional services. Thus it is an activity we know about, yet have trouble defining and weighing. The objective of this sourcebook is to make this ephemeral yet critically important topic a little more tangible—to define what it is and is not and to offer guidelines for the further process of defining and improving the quality of our efforts to serve our communities. As we see it, the key to this process is found in a systems approach.

One common barrier to effective consultation is found in the habit of many professionals of looking only at the person, group, system, or system level with which they are involved. We believe, rather, that we *must* be aware that a campus is a unique, definable system with many subsystems. Continuous attention to this basic fact, and recognition of the multiple effects of consulting with any one subsystem, are crucial for student services staff. Understanding the whole picture, in other words, is necessary no matter how small the intervention.

Though many professionals talk about *systems,* we believe that there is great inconsistency in the use of the term and in the use of the systems approach. As we see it, the unique contribution of this sourcebook is our proposal for using general systems theory as a theoretical framework with essentially unlimited applicability to consultation by student services staff. We encourage our readers to consider this approach so as to achieve greater cohesiveness in thinking, greater effectiveness in doing.

In addition, we will introduce the concept of *mediated services,* a term which includes consultation as well as other interventions serving the target population (students or others) by affecting individuals or groups who in turn affect the target population. Several authors use this concept; others retain the concept of consultation. Student services organizations may have different ideas about what they choose to include in their "consultation" area; we offer the new term as one coherent way to conceptualize indirect services.

Throughout this sourcebook, counseling centers are often used as examples or as model agencies for the topic being discussed. This reflects the professional identities of the authors. We have, however, attempted to make all chapters applicable to the majority of student services agencies, regardless of the particular example.

In the first chapter we outline major theories and models of consultation drawn from various realms. We then propose an approach using general systems theory to integrate relevant theory and technique within a cohesive, pragmatic model for student services staff.

One consistent concern about student services professionals as consultants is that of competence. Mary M. Leonard presents a model for training consultants which includes didactic and experiential components.

Evaluations are essential for defining and describing our work as consultants. There are few data but great demand by consumers who want information about results, and from ethical professionals who want to know the impact of their efforts. Stephen C. Paul summarizes relevant theory and practice to provide a starting point for consultants to assess their activities.

As student services staffs become more systems-oriented, it becomes increasingly necessary to acknowledge issues of politics, power, and ethics in consultation. James H. Banning, an ecologically oriented administrator, addresses such questions within the framework of an institutional change perspective.

The traditional differences between direct and indirect services may not be as important as we have thought in the past. We provide a model for organization of the mediated service function in student services organization, using a university counseling center as an example.

Though consultation/mediated services activities are growing in number and in scope, it is still a controversial question whether, or how much, we should be involved in them. James C. Hurst (in favor) and Harry Sharp (opposing) point out advantages and potential pitfalls of formal consultation for student services staff.

We conclude with some comments about the major issues in campus consultation and describe our hopes for the future. In addition, we note resource materials which we recommend most highly.

Preparing this issue of *New Directions for Student Services* has caused us to take a hard look at our own basic assumptions and values concerning student services in the area of consultation and beyond. It is our hope that the questions raised here (many of them unanswered) will be as stimulating to your thinking as they have been to ours, and that the suggestions provided will be useful.

M. Kathryn Hamilton
Charles J. Meade
Guest Editors

M. Kathryn Hamilton is senior psychologist at the University Counseling Center and assistant professor of psychology at Colorado State University.

Charles J. Meade is an assistant professor of counseling psychology and coordinator of consultation in the University Counseling Service at the University of Iowa.

*The college campus is a complex system which necessitates
the use of a variety of methods of intervention within
an integrated model of consultation.*

campus consultation:
toward a coherent
conceptualization

charles j. meade
m. kathryn hamilton

This chapter is an attempt to begin to systematically define the role of consultation within the field of student services in a university setting. As such, it is primarily concerned with the following issues:
- What do we *mean* when we talk about the activity of consultation; that is, what is a working definition of consultation?
- What are the important processes of consultation based on this working definition?
- What are the various models that currently exist which the consultant may use to act in a systematic fashion?
- Given the diversity of consultation models that exist, is there some conceptual framework so that the consultant has a coherent, internally consistent view of the nature of consulting?

Prior to addressing these issues, however, a brief overview of the historical impetus for consultation will be most helpful in order to understand the current issues.

background

Two major sources of impetus stand out as the most important factors in the development of consultation as a widely-practiced activity. These are the fields of industrial-organizational psychology and community psychology. Both these fields have stressed the importance of understanding the nature of human systems (for instance, business organizations, communities, and sub-cultures), and both have advocated that the behavioral scientist assume the role of consultant to these often large and complex groups of people as a way to deliver service efficiently and effectively (Blake and Mouton, 1976; Iscoe and Spielberger, 1970).

In terms of student affairs work on campus, the seminal piece is by Morrill, Oetting and Hurst (1974) which presented the now-famous "cube" of dimensions of counselor functioning in which "indirect service" (especially consultation) is seen as a very important function of student service personnel. The central theme of this article is that, as Caplan (1970) also argued, mental health (and by extension, student service) professionals ought to be more widely engaged in "prevention" rather than "cure"; the way to achieve that goal, according to this argument, was to intervene in the environment, making it a more healthy, supportive, and growth-producing atsmophere so that individuals could receive help from one another before their life problems became serious enough to warrant the attention of a professional therapist.

This approach to meeting human needs has been described as a "pyramid approach" (Archer and Kagan, 1973) because it envisions a few highly-trained professionals training a much larger number of "indigenous helpers" who then deliver service to a larger number of the actual target population. Training and consultation are two major activities of the professional in such an approach, while the direct service delivery is done by the trainees and consultees.

However, this view of "consultation" is limited compared to that of some authors from other disciplines (industrial-organizational psychology, community organization) or even from student services practitioners themselves (Huebner, 1977; Leonard's chapter in this volume). A very important first step, therefore, is to examine the various definitions of the term *consultation* and to attempt to arrive at one on which further discussion can be based.

definition of consultation

Previous Definitions. One of the earlier, most systematic definitions of consultation was provided by Lippitt (1959, p. 5): Consultation is "a general label for many variations of relationship" in which the following characteristics of the relationship are constant: (1) the relationship is a voluntary one between (2) a client system which needs help and professional helpers who (3) although they may belong to the client system, are definitely not part of the hierarchical power structure in which the client is located; (4) there is an attempt by the consultant to help the client solve a present or future problem; and (5) both the client and the consultant view the relationship as a temporary one which will end when both are satisfied that the problem has been satisfactorily resolved.

This definition views consultation as a *temporary, voluntary,* and *helping* relationship between an *expert* and a client which is *problem-focused.*

Another author (Gallesich, 1974, p. 138) has defined consultation as a "relationship in which an individual or an organization seeks professional services with the expectancy that consultative intervention will help solve work-related problems [in which] the consultee is free to reject any of the consultant's services and retains the power to terminate the relationship." There are two major foci in this definition: (1) it focuses on consultation as a problem-solving (remedial) activity; and (2) it is circumscribed by the world of work as the arena in which consultation occurs. From this point of view, the client may be anyone, from one person to an entire organization, and the definition assumes that the client requests the consultative intervention.

In their book on consultation, Blake and Mouton (1976, pp. 2-3) define consultation as *intervention* the purpose of which "is to help a person, a group, an organization or a larger social system identify and break out of [damaging cycles of behavior]." Thus, the consultant is seen as one who employs some strategy of intervention in a client system in order to help that client system to identify self-defeating and recurrent cyclical patterns and to adopt new, more productive patterns of behavior. It is obvious that this definition is broad enough to include everything from providing feedback on a colleague's research proposal to doing psychotherapy and, as such, sheds no light on the problem of *defining* consultation.

In sharp contrast to this very broad definition, Caplan (1970, p. 19) has provided a definition of mental health consultation which is quite limited in its scope, focusing on "a process of interaction between two professional persons — the consultant, who is a specialist, and the consultee, who invokes the consultant's help in regard to a current work problem with which he is having some difficulty and which he has decided is within the other's area of specialized competence." The consultant is viewed as a mental health professional, the consultee as a professional in mental health or some other field. The relationship is seen as more horizontal than vertical in most cases, although the consultant clearly is expected to have expertise in the particular area of concern. Interestingly, Caplan's notion of consultation assumes a dyadic unit as the basic one, whereas many others view the relationship as more variable in scope.

Consultation, then, is many things to many people. Such a state of affairs may not be terribly useful for the student services professional who is requested or instructed to "go out and consult with organization X about issue Y," particularly when said person may know little about organization X and even less about issue Y as it impacts organization X. One way to deal with this problem is to begin to define the activity of consultation in terms of the processes that are involved; that is, to define what it is that the consultant actually *does,* no matter which model one is working from (including no model at all).

A Working Definition. The following is offered as a definition which specifies the essential elements of effective consultation:

Consultation is a process in which the consultant (individual or group from outside of the immediate consultee system) utilizes expertise in human behavior to help the consultee (individual, group, or organization) to:

- assess the consultee's current level of functioning;
- generate strategies for maintaining or improving the consultee's functioning;
- make an informed decision on the consequences of implementing any given strategy;
- implement the apparently optimal strategy (which could, of course, mean no change from the current *modus operandi* of the consultee system);
- evaluate the effectiveness of the outcome (decision) of the consultation process; and
- terminate the consultative relationship once the desired outcome is attained and seems to be maintaining.

The above definition is a broad one which allows for "consultation" across many life areas from a preventive, developmental, and/or remedial framework. It specifies the essential elements of consultation which include entry and diagnosis, goal-directed (planning and strategizing) activity, decision-making and implementation of decisions, evaluation of and feedback into the consultee system, and termination after an appropriate time. This is done by a person who is either outside the system or who steps outside the system for the duration of the consultation in order to provide objectivity and low threat. Thus, this definition emphasizes the professional, systematic, and temporary nature of consultation. It is postulated that *all* of these activities must be included if consultation is to be a successful, meaningful activity producing positive, visible results which can be communicated to the consultee, the consultee's interested parties (including supervisors, administrators, and consumers), and the public. Consultation is defined as a systematic program of interventions occurring within a well-defined process and with clearly articulated goals and stages.

processes of consultation

Any systematic consultation endeavor has an orderly sequence so that one can define the stage of the process at any given time. For purposes of this chapter (as should be evident by now), consultation is viewed as an activity which occurs over time; thus, many activities which student services personnel might be inclined to call "consultation" (such as a one-shot talk to a group of residence hall assistants) would, from the perspective of this chapter, be seen as an event, occurring in one of the phases to be described below, of an overall consultative strategy. Without such an overall strategy, we would argue that something other than consultation is occurring (perhaps something such as "outreach" or some kind of "indirect service"). Interventions which are other than direct and for remediation are not necessarily "consultation" simply because they are not "direct service."

There are certain universal processes of consultation which must be systematically attended to. Each of these is examined in some detail below.

Entry. Before a consultative endeavor can even occur, the major task of entry into the consultee system must be achieved. Entry of an outsider into an organization is a complex affair, and the degree of success of the entry process has far-reaching implications for the success of the entire project. There are several forms of entry which may be differentiated, including:

1. Invited Entry. The consultee invites the consultant into the system, usually for the purpose of either remediating a problem or providing some form of "expert" input which the system lacks, even though there may be no defined problem. Such an invitation poses a number of questions for the consultant: the motivation of the consultee in making such a request, the nature of the target population (is it the person(s) who makes the request, some group under his or her supervision, the "organization" as a whole, . . . ?), the extent of autonomy the consultant will have, the degree to which the requestor (and/or client if they are different) understands the purpose of such a consultative relationship, and so on. Invited entry provides the consultant with a great deal of power and a huge opportunity to become a scapegoat if desirable outcomes are not attained. Usually, such an entry is requested as a reactive measure to remediate a problem, but it may be a request for either preventive or developmental input; in any case, clarification of the real purpose is crucial (see the section on assessment and diagnosis).

2. Uninvited Entry. The consultant initiates a relationship with a particular person or system for the purpose of either remediating a perceived problem in the consultee system, a perceived problem between the consultee and consultant systems, or for offering some expertise or service to the consultee. Such an invitation poses a new set of important issues for the consultant (some of which are relevant to invited entry), including an analysis of the consultant's motivations in initiating this action, the development of strategies for minimizing the potential for resistance due to such factors as territoriality and the consultee's perception of implicit criticism emanating from the consultant's approach, the consultant's utilization of consultee expertise in collaborative efforts, and determining the most accessible system level for effective entry to occur.

3. Mandated Entry. The consultant may enter a given system at the mandate of someone outside of that immediate system. This type of entry provides the consultant with a great deal of "legitimate power" and very little "referent power" and may well produce massive resistance on the part of the system being entered. It is sometimes not clear who the consultee *is* (the administrator or the system), and the power dynamics involved in such entry are intense and potentially destructive (see Sharp's chapter in this volume for a more detailed analysis of these issues).

4. Crisis Entry. While this may actually occur as one of the other three types, it merits special attention, since it occurs in response to a real or imagined crisis within the consultee system. In addition to the issues presented above, crisis entry demands that the consultant be well-versed in the dynamics

of individual and organizational reaction to crisis and be able to handle such response to the crisis. Given these dynamics, termination may be particularly abrupt and unresolved, leaving both the consultee and consultant feeling unfinished.

5. Accidental Entry. At times, the consultant may become involved in a system "by accident." Here the main danger is that the consultant may in fact become more involved in the system than he or she would have liked if the entry had been more planful.

These five different forms of entry into a consultee system, then, have very important implications for the direction that the consultation will take, particularly the phases which immediately follow.

Diagnosis. Assessment of the consultee system follows entry. The tasks of diagnosis have been alluded to in discussing the issues arising from the type of entry that has occurred. The consultant must begin to assess the conditions of the consultee system which will affect the process, such as client motives, the readiness of the client (system) for change, the central problems or issue(s) to be addressed, likely points of resistance, hidden agenda, strengths of the consultee (system), and so on. The process which takes place and the skills required are very similar to those which occur in counseling or dealing with an individual student about some personal issue. However, in working with an organization or group (including an informal organization such as a residence hall floor), the assessment skills required are often more complex and the task more demanding, particularly when that group is enmeshed in a hierarchical structure with a number of supra-systems (residence hall, residence hall system, student services, central administration, board of regents), all of whom may be very concerned with the issue surrounding the consultation. A thorough assessment, therefore, is critical in any major consultative undertaking and usually requires more subtle expertise than doing something like a straightforward survey.

Contracting. Once the assessment has been completed, contracting is the next crucial step. Establishing a contract with which both parties are satisfied may require large measures of patience, assertiveness, sensitivity to the underlying messages and agenda, flexibility, and more than a pinch of political savvy. A well-designed contract defines the responsibilities of both parties (in fact, defines the *identity* of both parties since it is often somewhat vague just who the client actually is), the expectations, goals, objectives, timetable, payment, and sanctions of the consultative relationship. It is often a good idea to have a written agreement, and it is very important to occasionally renew and/or renegotiate the contract if the relationship is long-term.

Data-Collection and Analysis. Renewal and/or renegotiation most often depend on data-collection and analysis. It is in this phase of the consultative relationship that the actual strategies for maintaining or improving the consultee functioning begin to crystallize, and the general goals get translated into specific behavioral objectives. One of the fundamental mistakes that a consultant can make is to implement a plan without having very solid data on which to base it. For example, in the unlikely event that a department head would call in some student affairs consultant (for instance, staff from the counseling center) to work toward helping the department resolve the problem of low morale among the graduate students and faculty, it would be folly to do anything without first having collected a lot of data, formally or informally, on the motivation for change among the various subgroups, the actual degree of dissatisfaction, the patterns of interaction which currently exist, the perceptions of the physical environment, the status of the department within the university, and so on. Such data can be collected unobtrusively or directly but are basic to informed planning and decision-making. In addition, if the data are collected carefully, it should be possible to anticipate certain unintended adverse consequences of implementing certain plans of action (Webb and others, 1966).

Implementation. After decisions have been reached by the consultant as to appropriate and/or alternate plans of action, the next phase is implementation. It is often at this point that the consultant will wish to form a team made up of various members of the consultee system (including the target population) for discussing the options and arriving at decisions as to appropriate intervention or nonintervention. At times, the team will have been formed earlier (for example, if the consultee specifically requests a diagnostic consultation it may be appropriate to use members from the system from the beginning to reduce the likelihood of resistance) but this may lead to conflict among team members about how to diagnose the problem. It is, however, essential to develop a working team in time to assist with actually putting the plan into operation.

Evaluation. Evaluating the result of the consultative intervention is crucial from both a scientific and a practical viewpoint. The evaluation process is discussed in detail elsewhere (see Paul's chapter in this volume) and these comments will be brief. From the consultant's perspective, evaluation should be seen as an information feedback process which actually begins with entry (formative evaluation) and continues throughout the time of the project until the final product is being evaluated (summative evaluation). Oetting and Cole (1977) have provided a helpful "cookbook" approach to evaluation; the consultant should take pains to design an evaluation system which gives prompt information (feedback which allows for change in midstream if necessary) and which is appropriate in terms of rigor for the kind of consultation being undertaken.

Termination. Once the goals and objectives of the project have been achieved, the last step in the process, termination, occurs. It is a delicate, important process which requires sensitivity to both emotional and pragmatic aspects of the consultant and consultee. It is often tempting for counselors to carry a client who is ready for termination if the client is enjoyable and continuing to profit from counseling; similarly, it is tempting to continue a consultative relationship if it is enjoyable and productive. Most models of consultation, however, stress the importance of building in the termination process from the entry stage on, so that the consultee can be prepared to take what the consultant has to offer and to adapt it to his or her system and style. The consultation has been successful, then, to the degree that a satisfactory termination has been achieved such that the consultee no longer needs the consultant. As a rule, consultation is a time-limited event with a clear entry and termination point.

Processes as Contents in Consultation. As with a counseling relationship, the process rather than the content of interaction may become the focus of discussion in a consultative relationship. Such an event is a two-edged sword and must be handled with care. Consultation is clearly not counseling or therapy; it does not aim at establishing an intense (transference) relationship and is not set up along the same power dynamics as therapy (the participants remain equals). Therefore it is imperative that the consultant steer a course which is challenging and likely to produce change but which avoids the danger of stimulating strong transference or resistance.

One potential hazard is to overtly attend to the process of personal interactions in the consultant/consultee relationship. This is likely to intensify the relationship dynamics. It would be better to view the process (in each of its stages) as part of the diagnostic data. Thus, relationship dynamics are dealt with covertly, and difficulties encountered in the consultative relationship may well throw light on the basic problems of the client.

This set of processes, then, is at one and the same time a conceptual definition of consultation, the operational definition of effective consultation, the temporal framework for the consultative relationship, and a diagnostic aid regarding the consultee system. It is by no means a complete model but does provide a frame of reference for model-building, a task to which this chapter shall now turn.

models and metaphors

There is currently no universal, well-constructed *theory* of consultation, particularly in a college or university setting. There are, rather, a number of *models* of consultation, some of them more or less applicable to the college setting. All of these models can serve as heuristic devices for practitioners and administrators in grappling with the role of consultation on campus today and in the future. These models come from industrial-organizational psychology (Blake and Mouton, 1976; Porter, Lawler, and Hackman, 1975), community organization (Alinsky, 1972), community mental health (Caplan, 1970), organizational development and human relations work (Schein, 1969), and counseling psychology (Blocher, 1975).

Current Models of Consultation. Probably the major field of study which has provided us with a model of consultation is industrial-organizational psychology. There are several currently well-accepted models of consultation within that field. Porter, Lawler, and Hackman (1975) have provided a framework for understanding the consultation process which relies heavily on traditional theory of formal organizations. In this approach to consultation, the organization is usually viewed as the client, and the consultant's task is to elucidate the role which various properties of the organization (administrative structure, lines of communication and decision-making, economic structure, organizational climate) play in the overall functioning of the system. The aim of the consultant is to assist the organization in achieving its tasks and objectives. The emphasis is on task performance, individual performance as it intersects with organizational goals, and on the structure of the organization as it affects performance. The major benefit of such an approach for the student service professional is to clarify the importance of formal organizational structure in determining organizational effectiveness.

Using a very different approach, but one which is still somewhat within the purview of organizational psychology, Blake and Mouton (1976) have developed a model which they call the "consulcube." This quantifies the three dimensions of any consultation intervention: the target population, in five steps from individual to larger social systems; five possible methods of intervention (acceptant, catalytic, confrontation, prescriptive, and theoretical); and four purposes of intervention (power/authority, morale/cohesion, norms/standards, goals/objectives). Thus there are $5 \times 5 \times 4$ or 100 squares within the cube which may be analyzed according to the target, purpose, and method of the intervention (very reminiscent of the "cube" of Morrill, Oetting, and Hurst, 1974). The model is very pragmatic and enables practitioners to make informed decisions about the kind of strategy to use at a given point but does little to enable them to make the early decisions at entry, diagnosis, and contracting phases about the most appropriate course of action. It is an implementation rather than a decision model (as opposed to Porter, Lawler, and Hackman who emphasize organizational diagnosis).

A third approach to consultation which is often employed is Schein's (1969) process consultation model. This grew out of the early work of the National Training Laboratories (NTL) and the "human relations" approach to dealing with individual and organizational change. Here the consultant has one major task, to help the consultee understand the "process" of human interaction and task accomplishment. This process includes interpersonal dynamics such as power and influence, group dynamics such as coalition-building and intergroup conflict, the dynamics of change, and so on. The goals of the consultant include generating valid information, promoting free and informed choice on the part of the consultee, and encouraging the consultees to make an internal commitment to the choices they make. The assumptions of the process consultation model are somewhat humanistic in flavor. It is assumed that most organizations could be more effective if they could identify the psychological or group processes that need improvement; that every organization has strengths and weaknesses and will be committed to realizing its potential; and that it is best if the client arrives at his or her own solutions.

A very different approach to consultation has been outlined by Caplan (1970) which he calls "mental health consultation." This model describes a role for the consultant which may occur within a context of primary, secondary, or tertiary prevention in which the consultant, a mental health expert, engages in a quasi-supervisory relationship with another professional. The intervention may be of four types: client-centered case consultation (most similar to traditional supervision); consultee-centered case consultation (also similar to traditional supervision); program-centered administrative consultation (what is the agency to do with this issue); and consultee-centered administrative consultation (in which the organization is the client and organizational problems are the issue). The model is clearly most appropriate for student service agencies which are mental health units, such as the counseling center.

Blocher (1975) provides a model which he calls a "systematic eclectic approach." The model is really an atheoretical one which draws from a number of counseling, training, and consultation systems within the field of psychology. There are techniques from human relations training, group processes, social psychology, and learning theory. The temporal sequence of consultation is well outlined through a series of nine steps from defining the agency's goals through evaluating and providing feedback to the consultee. The model is very much a "teaching" model of consultation in which the consultant takes an active role in modeling and shaping behavior; at times, it is unclear whether this approach is actually a *training* model as opposed to a *consultation* model.

Finally, as an example of a very different conceptualization of consultation, Alinsky (1972) has proposed an advocacy model which deals directly with the political and power issues involved in working with traditionally powerless groups. The consultant works toward helping such groups develop strategies for obtaining power, usually by identifying and training indigenous leaders and then operating "behind the scenes" to help the group coalesce and move toward an action plan. Clearly, this approach to consultation is the most potentially explosive and dangerous for an agency to engage in. But it may also be one of the most necessary for student services personnel, since it is often students or student subgroups who are powerless within the university system.

Such diversity is both exciting and frustrating. The consultant who is familiar with all of these approaches has at his or her fingertips a wealth of information and conceptual systems to use in consulting work. At the same time, however, with such an array of approaches available it is easy to become lost in all of the trees and to lose sight of the forest such that the strategies of intervention become dependent on the model which is used. It would be better to choose an appropriate model (with accompanying strategies) based on a set of super-ordinate goals and assumptions concerning the role of consultation in a college or university system.

A recent survey (Hamilton, 1978) has illustrated the dilemma very well. The results indicate that while almost all college counseling centers say they are engaged in "consultation," the term is used to encompass almost any kind of "nontraditional" service. In most cases, formal training in consultation has been spotty at best; the models employed are either nonexistent or those someone on the staff has encountered at some point in their professional development (usually informally and briefly). Informal contacts indicate that a similar situation exists in other student service agencies. This is not to imply that the consultation done is necessarily *bad,* but that at this point there is no coherent conceptualization of the consultative endeavor in student services on campus today.

What is required is a metaphor, a general model of the consultative enterprise in a complex system such as the university which is at once independent of but consistent with the more limited views of consultation which have been developed by other disciplines. Such a metaphor should provide a gestalt, an overview, which enables the practitioner to choose from already existing models of consultation, to tailor the generic processes of consultation outlined above to the particular consultative project of interest, and to retain the view of the forest while attending to the individual trees. The metaphor is probably currently best articulated in the body of thought known as general system theory and the view it provides of the world, "the systems view."

General System Theory. A general theory of systems was first proposed by Bertalanffy (1950) as an attempt to develop "the formulation and derivation of those principles which are valid for 'systems' in general . . . we find that models, principles, and laws exist which apply to generalized systems irrespective of their particular kind, elements, and 'forces' involved" (Bertalanffy, 1968, pp. 32–33). What the system theorists propose is to specify the kinds of interactions which exist in any given system and to identify regularities in those patterns of interactions across all systems.

The first task is to define the term *system.* Vickers (1970) has defined a system as a regulated set of elements and their relationships to each other and to the set as a whole. Bertalanffy (1950) has similarly defined a system as a complex of interacting elements, specifically elements P, which stand in relations R, such that the behavior of some element P in R is different from the behavior of P in R '.

Perhaps several brief examples can clarify. A system may be any collection of components which interact: thus, a family is a system; so is an organization, a team, a machine, an ecosystem, a university. Systems may contain subsystems and be contained by suprasystems. A student services organization such as a resident life system has subsystems (particular dormitories) and is contained by other systems (student affairs, the university). The resident life system interacts with these subsystems and suprasystems in a regulated way; however, it also interacts with other systems (food service, counseling center, student activities office) which are at once independent of resident life yet also subsystems of the larger systems such as the division of student affairs.

This interaction with the environment (other systems) defines an *open* system (because it is open to exchange of energy and information from and to the "environment" as opposed to a *closed* system, such as a chemical reaction which occurs entirely within a closed container). Open systems have a number of unique properties; Katz and Kahn (1966) list a number of them, including:

1. Input: intake of energy or information from the environment.
2. Throughput: transformation of the input.
3. Output: exportation of some product or behavior to the environment.

4. Systems as cycles of events: the first three elements combined produce a continuous flow between the system and the environment, and interruption of the cycle at any of the three points produces disruption in the entire cycle.
5. Negative entropy: the system develops toward a state of higher order and greater differentiation (it becomes more ordered and more complex).
6. Coding and negative feedback: coding is a way of categorizing the input so that it takes on meaning; negative feedback is the process of self-correction so that the system maintains its orderly transaction with the environment.

The remaining characteristics, dynamic homeostasis, differentiation, and equifinality are beyond the scope of this chapter except to note that a system will tend toward remaining in a "steady-state" and be unlikely to change unless there is massive internal or external fluctuation.

Another important concept related to systems is the notion of a *boundary*. The boundary of a system, according to Chin (1976a), is that visible or invisible line which separates a system from its environment such that there is a greater exchange of energy and information *within* the boundary than there is *across* it. He has further pointed out (1976b) that any effective strategy for change of a system requires that one locate the system/environment boundary, especially so that the "environment" can be analyzed in terms of the forces it exerts on the system and the "system" can be analyzed in terms of the manner in which it interacts with the environment. Boundaries of systems may be more or less defined and observable, more or less permeable, and more or less flexible. Often the boundaries of subsystems of universities are very diffuse and intangible. For example, where is the boundary of the office of student activities, since usually student activities cut across most of the other subsystems in the university — since, in fact, that is part of the *role* of the office of student activities? It requires careful analysis to locate the boundary of some system or subsystem, particularly in a large and multileveled complex system such as a university.

It is the position of this chapter that the most useful way to think about a consulting activity emanating from a student affairs agency is that it involves one part of the university (for instance, counseling center, evaluation and examination service) impacting another part of that university (for instance, academic department, residence hall), and that it is *absolutely essential* to understand how each of these parts perceive that larger system as well as how they perceive one another. Several authors have pointed out that the "environment" of a system is that which is relatively "fixed," that over which the system has little control (Chin, 1976b; Churchman, 1968). *The* key question which the student affairs consultant must ask is: "Does the consultee system see me as part of the environment, as a subsystem of the same overall system and thus subject to the same environment, or as some combination of these two positions?" The answer to this fundamental question will determine almost all of the potential aspects of the consultative relationship, from entry issues through termination, from the question of whether *consultation* is actually being done to the choice of the most appropriate model of consultation.

Intersystems and Subsystems. Chin (1976a) has proposed an important differentiation between an intersystem model (two open systems connected to each other) and a subsystem model (two sub-units of some larger system). As he points out (p. 96), there are two essential differences which are captured in the distinction: "We may lose the critical fact of the autonomy of the components, or the direct interactional or transactional consequences for the separate components when we treat the sub-systems as merely parts of a larger system. The intersystem model exaggerates the virtues of autonomy and the limited nature of interdependence of the interactions between the two connected systems." That is, two open systems are autonomous and only mildly interdependent, whereas two subsystems are, by virtue of being merely parts of a larger system, relatively nonautonomous and highly interdependent.

Traditionally, models of consultation have assumed that the consultant is from outside of the consultee system, thereby ensuring that he or she would have a kind of independence, perspective, and objectivity that would be unattainable for someone from within the system. This is, of course, the "consultant as expert" model, which carries with it an often-overlooked corollary, namely the "consultant as objective observer." All of the models which have been discussed earlier take it as a given that the consultant has *no vested interest* in the functioning of the consultee system but, rather, serves as a "provider of service" for professional, ethical, or monetary reasons (or some combination).

However, the entire equation changes when the consultant is part of the *same* system. Internal consultants are, by definition, set apart from yet still a part of the "consultee" system. This places the campus consultee system in a dire dilemma: the boundaries of the system (agency), so important in maintaining its identity and defining input and output, are suddenly extremely unclear. The system "feels" in danger of being swallowed up, of losing its identity, of being subsumed by a subsystem which *competes* for resources within the overall system (recall that "resources" include all of the within-system things of value, from cash and equipment to "good will" and type of personnel). The question arises: in asking that a campus unit which perceives itself as a (co-equal) subsystem of the college or university request/submit to ongoing "consultation" from another unit, are we in fact asking the consultee unit to subject itself to feeling that it is risking its identity and equal status?

The answer is: it all depends. It depends on a number of factors which must be attended to in any systems analysis, factors such as the stress within the system, the conflicts between subsystems, the forces pushing the units together, the degree of congruence among subsystems' goals and objectives, the system rewards and punishments for cooperation or competition, and so on. While the answer is not terribly complex, the analysis *is* complex and demands a high level of skill on the part of the consultant.

implications of the system perspective for campus consultation

The most fundamental implication of the system perspective for working in campus consultation is to remember that the university is a multi-level system. It is absolutely essential to define the level at which consultative activity should intervene. Consultation must include specifying the level of the target within the consultant's system and the relationship between the consultee and the consultant system. It is not enough to specify the target (individual, group, organization); it is necessary to specify the consultant/target relationship, the interface between the two systems.

For example, let us suppose that a member of the counseling center presents a workshop on depression. The target group of such a presentation might be a single residence hall, the residence hall system, or the student services administration. Clearly, the target group taken in isolation determines to some extent the nature of the consultative endeavor; but an equally if not more important determinant is the nature of the relationship between the consultant and consultee system. If entry into the system is desired as a result of the intervention, then careful attention to the (intersystem or subsystem) dynamics is required.

This is similar to yet different from the purpose of the intervention. The purpose may be to impact the consultee's environment, system, or system-environment interactions. It would be possible to work toward any of these purposes with any of the three groups mentioned in the example. But the manner in which the achievement of the purpose is attempted will vary considerably depending on: (1) the consultant's definition of the relationship between his or her system and the consultee system; (2) the consultee's view of same; and (3) the consultant's perception of the consultee's view of same. In essence, then, the systems view requires that the consultant specify where his or her system is *vis-a-vis* the consultee's system and that the consultant specify how he or she thinks the consultee views the relationship. It is only the resolution of this issue which will lead to a determination of entry strategy.

Many consultants view their difficulties with entry in terms of the resistance of the system being approached or entered, and surely that is a factor. Yet a careful assessment of the issues outlined above could ease the difficulties immensely. An example may be helpful to illustrate this point.

Consultation Within Student Services. Let us suppose that one student services agency (for instance—as is often the case—the counseling center) wishes to consult with another agency (for example the residence hall system) about mutual concerns of student mental health and development. The entry could be made from two models, the intersystem or the subsystem models proposed by Chin (1976a). The intersystem model views the two agencies as autonomous units, the subsystem model sees them as two subunits of student services. These two models have quite different implications for the kind of consultation effort that could be expected.

The subsystem model would be most likely to raise immediate issues of dependence/counterdependence, since both of the agencies are viewed as part of the larger student services system. The inclination is to either form a coalition to increase power within the larger system (dependence) or, on the other hand, to compete against one another for resources within the larger system (counterdependence). The intersystem model, on the other hand, views the two agencies as autonomous interdependent units who have their own strengths and weaknesses and who may wish to engage in mutual consultation which is quite different from the collaboration encouraged by the subsystem model.

If the subsystem approach is chosen, entry issues become very confused since it is uncertain whether the consultant and consultee are already *in* the same system, thereby negating the need for entry to be made at all! The intersystem approach clearly articulates entry as a major factor in the development of a consultative relationship. In addition, the content areas are less clear with the subsystem model than with the intersystem view: subsystems are likely to see themselves in a frame of "since we're both student services agencies we both have similar expertise across dimensions" whereas the intersystem thinker would argue that "we have areas of great and of little common interest, and I have a different kind of expertise than you have — how can you use my expertise for your system?"

One other very important difference between the two models is in the articulation of the environment. Subsystems see themselves as having different environments with some overlap. A belief in *common* environment may quickly lead to an agreement that both put on the same spectacles (and thus share the same distortions). Acknowledgement of *different* environments creates the opportunity for objectivity. Two systems do not have the "same" environment and do not pretend that they do. Two subsystems do have (almost) the same environment.

Consultation is not collaboration. The student services professional who consults within the division with other units may be inclined to take a "we're all in this together" approach to encourage cooperation. However, in the long run such an approach is fraught with dangers. Consultation is cooperative when the consultant provides some expertise unique to him or her with the intention of providing service. Student service agencies can (and should) consult with one another, but if the maximum benefit is to be obtained, the relationship should be seen as mutually interdependent and the consultations themselves should be completely independent of one another.

The same general issues apply to consultation with outside units (like academic departments) except that the interdependence (as opposed to mutual dependence) is usually much clearer and the expertise of the consultant usually more clearly acknowledged and valued. Here the intersystem model is the only one that makes sense. Consulting with administrators should also, in our view, be approached from an intersystem perspective, with the consultant (let us say an expert on depression and suicide) working with a system within the university (in this case administrators) who have mutual interests but different expertise. But, as noted earlier, the manner in which the actual consulting is approached could vary to some extent (in fact, *must* vary to some extent) since the mutual interests and unique expertise vary from residence hall personnel to administrators, thus *inherently* defining the relationship between consultant and consultee differently.

Clarifying the relationship (subsystem or intersystem) between consultant and consultee provides the framework for the entire task. Each view demands a particular approach to consultation which is quite different from the other. In general, the intersystem view provides greater objectivity and less resistance after entry and is more congruent with the models of consultation presented here. However, there are times when the subsystem perspective is closer to reality and is appropriate. The particular view one adopts will have important implications for the type of consultation chosen.

summary

Systems thinking provides a conceptual overview for the consultative enterprise and gives the consultant an array of questions and strategies for impacting and assisting other systems. Once certain parameters are clear, an informed choice can be made about the appropriate model to use, planning can be done to maximize the potential benefit of each of the stages for the consultee, the limits of the relationship can be articulated and appreciated, and various areas of expertise can be unified in order to provide better service to the entire university system (and, by extension, to the larger community). The consultative process is aided considerably by an awareness of the autonomous and interdependent nature of the multiple systems within the university.

references

Alinsky, S. D. *Rules for Radicals.* New York: Random House, 1972.

Archer, J., and Kagan, N. "Teaching Interpersonal Relationship Skills on Campus: A Pyramid Approach." *Journal of Counseling Psychology,* 1973, *20,* 535–540.

Bertalanffy, L. von. "An Outline of General System Theory." *British Journal of Philosophy of Science,* 1950, *1,* 139–164.

Bertalanffy, L. von. *General System Theory: Foundation, Development, Applications.* New York: George Braziller, 1968.

Blake, R. R., and Mouton, J. S. *Consultation.* Reading, Mass.: Addison-Wesley, 1976.

Blocher, D. H. "A Systematic Eclectic Interventional Model." In C. Parker (Ed.), *Psychological Consultation: Helping Teachers With Special Needs.* Reston, Va.: The Council for Exceptional Children, 1975.

Caplan, G. *The Theory and Practice of Mental Health Consultation.* New York: Basic Books, 1970.

Chin, R. "The Utility of Systems Models and Development Models for Practitioners." In W. G. Bennis and others (Eds.), *The Planning of Change.* New York: Holt, Rinehart and Winston, 1976a.

Chin, R. "The Utility of Models of the Environments of Systems for Practitioners." In W. G. Bennis and others (Eds.), *The Planning of Change.* New York: Holt, Rinehart and Winston, 1976b.

Churchman, C. W. *The Systems Approach.* New York: Delacourt Press, 1968.

Gallesich, J. "Training the School Psychologist for Consultation." *Journal of School Psychology,* 1974, *12* (2), 138–149.

Hamilton, M. K. "Survey of Consultation Activities in College Counseling Centers." Fort Collins: University Counseling Center, Colorado State University, 1978.

Huebner, L. A. "Counseling Interventions: An Organizational-Interactional Approach." *The Counseling Psychologist*, 1977, *7* (2), 69–73.

Iscoe, I., and Spielberger, C. D. *Community Psychology: Perspectives in Training and Research*. New York: Appleton-Century-Crofts, 1970.

Katz, D., and Kahn, R. L. *The Psychology of Organizations*. New York: Wiley, 1966.

Lippitt, R. "Dimensions of the Consultant's Job." *Journal of Social Issues*, 1959, *15* (2), 5–12.

Morrill, W. H., Oetting, E. R., and Hurst, J. C. "Dimensions of Counselor Functioning." *Personnel and Guidance Journal*, 1974, *52* (b), 355–359.

Oetting, E. R., and Cole, C. W. "Method, Design, and Implementation in Evaluation." In G. Hanson (Ed.), *New Directions for Student Services: Evaluating Program Effectiveness*, no. 1. San Francisco: Jossey-Bass, 1978.

Porter, L. W., Lawler, E. E., and Hackman, J. R. *Behavior in Organizations*. New York: McGraw-Hill, 1975.

Schein, E. *Process Consultation: Its Role in Organizational Development*. Reading, Mass.: Addison-Wesley, 1969.

Vickers, G. "A Classification of Systems." *General Systems*, 1970, *15*, 3–6.

Webb, E. J., and others. *Unobtrusive Measures: Nonreactive Research in the Social Sciences*. Chicago: Rand McNally, 1966.

M. Kathryn Hamilton is senior psychologist at the University Counseling Center and assistant professor of psychology at Colorado State University. In the counseling center, she is coordinator of mediated services and is actively involved in therapy, supervision, and research. In the psychology department, she teaches community psychology and seminars on selected personality topics. Her applied and academic activities reflect her current attempts at resolving the conflict (shared by many) of being a traditionally trained practitioner with a commitment to prevention and to working with systems.

Charles J. Meade is assistant professor of counseling psychology and coordinator of consultation in the University Counseling Service at the University of Iowa. This dual role has provided him with the vexing challenge of integrating consultation theory and practice into a meaningful whole.

*If good training of campus consultants is to be accomplished,
one must incorporate a number of didactic
and experiential components in a model which captures
the complexity of consultation in the college setting.*

training consultants

mary m. leonard

Many of the same issues that face student service personnel in delivering consultative services also face those who are engaged in the process of training consultants. These issues include the environmental and political conditions on campus which are essential to success in *doing* consultation, which is viewed here as an essential element in *training* in consultation. In the first portion of this chapter, several of these conditions are discussed, particularly in terms of the difficulties they pose for training. Subsequently, a model of training is presented which attempts to sensitize trainees to the complexities and vagaries of consultation through a combination of didactic, experiential, and actual field training experiences. Finally, several recommendations are offered for overcoming obstacles to formalizing training in consultation.

environmental conditions

Training in consultation is most often a by-product of substantial amounts of consultation work accomplished by a talented staff. By the time an organization gets to the level of training others in consultation skills, most of the necessary-but-not-sufficient environmental variables which determine whether or not much consultation work occurs on a campus have been addressed. These central environmental variables are: structure of the work place in which the consultation is done, degree to which the campus is informed, and political issues involved in doing consultation on a college campus. These variables contribute to the amount, kind, and quality of consultation and training that are done. If any of these variables are overlooked, reactive and problem oriented student services are more apt to dominate a campus.

Informed Campus. The overall campus "gestalt" with respect to consultative activities is an important factor in doing and training in consultation. The receptivity of the campus to consultation, the availability of trainees and supervisors, and the ability to integrate consultation training with formal coursework all contribute to the kind and amount of consultative service and training that occurs in an educational community. If the campus has a history of distrust of mental health and student development services, sees its mission as solely academic, or is absorbed in survival issues, then it will be difficult to implement a sound program of consultative activity and training.

Systematic training in consultation is particularly affected by the overall campus climate, since, in order for comprehensive training to occur, a campus must have: (1) trainees who are interested in and encouraged by their departments or employers to receive formal training in consultation; (2) trainers who have academic credentials, experience in consultation, and an operating base; and (3) professionals who consult regularly and who are able and willing to provide supervision. Occasionally (for example, in a counseling center or student activities office) there is an entire system geared up to train consultants and no trainees because the relevant academic departments emphasize reactive modes of service delivery.

For the student service professional(s) who attempt to develop a systematic training program it is essential to get a reading on the campus climate as it is likely to impact availability of resources, including trainees, and on the potential for integrating training activities into the academic structures on campus. In addition, the ability to implement a thorough training program may well depend on the ability to *create* an informed campus through "educational" interventions directed toward specific groups on campus. Besides the overall campus environment, there are important variables in individual campus agencies which must also be considered.

Structure of the Work Place. This is an environmental factor which is critical for achieving quality consultative services. Since consultation may well originate from a number of places, including academic, student service, or administrative departments, it may be that the type of work place will determine the manner in which some of the structural issues discussed below are addressed. However they are resolved, though, several variables of the work environment are especially important to consider.

The first of these conditions is the mission statement and hiring practices of the consulting agency. Consultation goals and training need to be built into the structure of the organization. Sometimes the consultation work of the organization is relegated to a few members who are particularly interested and committed to it. The advantage of this approach is having staff doing the work they prefer and doing it well. The disadvantage is that remaining staff stay unknowledgeable and unskilled in consultation work and unavailable for consultation supervision. What seems optimal in a given system is to neither ghetto-ize the staff who do consultation work nor mandate that all staff do consultation. The whole system needs to *decide* how much consultation work and training it wants to assume in conjunction with its other missions. Trainees then can see firsthand how an organization can determine its goals, allocate its resources, assign personnel and fulfill its mission. When trainees go to other organizations which might be grappling with the issue of balancing consultation work with the other foci of the organization, the trainee has a model to conceptualize alternative solutions if he or she has seen the process of decision-making in action.

A second important element of the agency workings to consider is the way in which work time is conceptualized. Proactive consultation work often requires the availability of large chunks of open time to allow the consultant to respond quickly to issues which invariably come up and need to be addressed immediately. This requires a flexible system which can provide compensatory time for work which often needs to be done evenings and weekends, a particularly difficult problem for an agency such as a counseling center which tends to function on a 50-minute hour schedule. It also presents trainees with demands on their time which may, on occasion, seem *overly* demanding.

The third major structural element which affects training in consultation is whether resources are provided for it. It is often difficult enough to obtain resources for doing consultation, but training others in it is a fairly time-consuming process which is likely to show more long-term rather than short-term benefits. When a counseling center or student affairs vice president's office is faced with responding to a high demand for direct service, it is difficult to commit a lot of resources in time and energy to an activity such as consultation, but such a commitment must be there if high quality training is to occur.

political issues

Territoriality among campus groups and consultants' multiple relationships with students, staff and faculty highlight the major campus political issues facing the trainer of consultants.

Territoriality. Issues of territoriality may arise among academic departments, offices in student affairs, and student organizations. Competition for clients signals the growing interest among some professionals whose preferred mode of intervention is consultation intervention. The competition and territoriality issues can evolve out of different values, the desire to be influential, the interest in increasing student numbers in classes, and fear of budget cuts. These variables should be discussed with trainees to help them conceptualize the campus student service community, begin proactive interventions, and to prepare them to deal with similar difficulties on other campuses they are likely to encounter.

As an example of the value issues that may emerge in a political context, consider the case of a faculty member who complains of students' lack of responsiveness in class, poor quality in their examinations, and high drop-out rate from the class. Solutions to these problems might well vary according to the agency involved and particular orientation of consultation: the reading and study skills expert may focus on students' skills; the deliberate psychological education instructor would likely deal with matching the curriculum with students' moral or cognitive development; an evaluation service consultant may work at evaluating teacher effectiveness; a counseling psychologist may be inclined to treat the entire classroom as a system and intervene at that level. While all of these interventions could have value, the reality is that in all likelihood at most one would be implemented, which would largely depend on issues of politics and territory: The type of coordination necessary to produce an integrated approach to campus consultation does not occur often and until various disciplines and levels of the university system engage in such coordination territoriality is likely to continue.

Trainees must face this reality in a number of situations and must learn to deal with it in a number of ways. Consultants are faced with difficult and complex political realities which occur within the college or university community. To analyze the previous example: the selection of the target population (students, teacher, or entire class) may, in part, be a volatile political issue; attempting to coordinate consultative efforts among interacting systems presents one with power and competency dynamics which are potent and must be dealt with sensitively; issues of power dynamics within the classroom are immediately present (consultant serving as student advocate *vs.* professor advocate *vs.* mediator); the role of student service professional consulting with an academic department presents interesting issues concerning expertise in education (even if the professor is open to receiving such consultation, what will his or her colleagues say about it?). One of the central tasks of a training program in consultation is to provide trainees with experience in dealing with these values and political questions.

Too Many Hats. The consultant on a college campus often is in the position of wearing a number of different hats at different times (faculty member, counselor, administrator, student advocate, consultant to central administration). If he or she is not careful about keeping the roles as separate as possible, chaos can result. The consultant may feel pressure from a number of groups to get certain agenda run and may, in fact, feel some personal investment in a plan of action being implemented when wearing one hat (as faculty) and feel compelled to maintain a kind of objectivity when wearing another (as consultant to a department). Multiple roles present multiple problems, and trainees must be helped to deal with all of the multiplicity in some way.

The multiplicity expands when one realizes that trainees are students who may well be in a program which has a direct relationship with another program or agency with whom they are consulting (for example, a college student personnel doctoral student consulting out of a counseling center with an assistant vice president for student services and faculty member from the student's program). Conversely, the consultee may be a graduate student in the program in which the consultant is a faculty member. The consultant/

faculty member may acquire information about the consultee/student which could have a major impact on the student's progress in the program. It is imperative that these kinds of issues be understood by trainers and dealt with by trainees if the program is to succeed.

In summary, the process of training consultants can be seen as a complex affair which depends, in part, on a number of conditions on the campus. With a university or college system, the multiple layers of the system and the multiple roles of the consultant/trainer within that system can be problematic. In addition, many campuses are enmeshed in a web of ideas of service delivery which focus on remediation and on the individual student, a situation which leads to 90% of service delivery directed toward 10% of the population (Blocher, 1973). In the following section, a training model is presented which has been developed in part to deal with these issues as well as to present an optimal learning environment and sequence of developmental tasks for trainees.

a model for training consultants

The training model described below developed out of three conditions present on a university campus: a counseling department course on consultation theory, a supervised practicum in consultation in the university counseling center, and a high degree of cooperation between faculty, administrators and practitioners in these two settings. Modifications of this model are readily possible to fit diverse environments such as community, junior and state colleges or various student services offices. Originally this model was designed to train graduate students in counseling and psychology to do consultation. The model has expanded to include an internship and an inservice component for clinicians, academicians and administrators interested in cultivating new consultation skills.

The training model consists of three primary elements—the course, a supervised practicum and an internship in consultation. These three elements form the major components of the outline below. A fourth section has been added to suggest briefly ways in which the training may be modified for use with other training populations, as in inservice training. Most attention is devoted to presenting the course here, since any training program in consultation requires a good knowledge base on the part of the trainees. It is anticipated that the content could be obtained in other ways than through formal coursework; it is suggested that any systematic training program should include many of the elements presented here.

The basic training in consultation that has been developed includes five major components: the analysis of trainees' assumptions and values; major theories of consultation; generic steps in the consultation process; issues in consulting; and skills which the consultant must possess. Each of these will be discussed in detail below.

Assumptions and Values. The trainees' awareness of their own assumptions and values is a basic (and often covert) issue which must be addressed in a training program. How trainees view the world in general determines what they are likely to see as consultants. Psychologists, counselors, and other student services professionals have blinders which determine what they see and are not likely to see as foci of psychological interventions. The focus here will be on the major blinders of psychologists and counselors, although they may well carry over to others such as administrators and academicians (who may also have their own unique sets).

There are three such blinders which are particularly relevant here: *first,* the tendency of psychological approaches towards understanding people to focus on individuals, on problems, and on the past rather than on working with groups and systems on developmental and preventative interventions (Drum and Fiegler, 1973; Snow and Newton, 1976); *second,* the difficulty that many student service professionals have in transcending personal boundaries of race, sex, and class (Leonard and Collins, in press; Nutt, in press); and *third,* a reactive, nine-to-five mentality among many service deliverers (for example, staff of counseling centers, career services, reading and study skills laboratories). The overall effect of these blinders has been to work with individuals (primarily with "Y.A.V.I.S." *y*oung, *v*erbal, *i*ntelligent, *s*uccessful clients) (Bergin and Garfield, 1971), to view those from other life styles (gay persons providing a good example) as "sick" by definition (Brown, 1973), and to refrain from going out into the larger community and attempting to effect change.

This model of consultation proposes that these blinders be put aside and that new priorities be established, including an emphasis on prevention and development, targeting such interventions toward groups and organizations, and dealing with areas such as the economic, political, and educational realms when they are of most concern to the consultation clients. Trainees must be encouraged to examine their own biases and blinders along these dimensions; to do so, laboratory exercises can be particularly helpful.

Theories of Consultation. The foundation for training in consultation skills is laid by an examination of five general theories which cover different approaches to doing consulting. The focus here examines what these theories "do best" in consultation and why they are included in a consultation theory class. What needs to be underlined is that none of these models of consultation can be followed in an identical manner. Each theory makes distinct assumptions concerning the nature of humans, how people learn, and how change occurs (Bennis and others, 1976; Leonard, 1977). The five theories examined are those of Caplan (1964), Blocher (1975), Alinsky (1972), Huebner (1977), and Schein (1969).

Caplan's (1964) medical/expert approach is extremely useful for those situations in which the client-centered and program-centered consultation methods should be used. Caplan's model has molded many current attitudes, values and methods of consultation and is sometimes the sole model taught today to social workers, psychiatrists and traditionally trained clinical psychologists. Trainees need this perspective to understand other professionals' conceptual views of consultation in order to maximize cooperation and understanding interdisciplinary team work. In addition, this model can be used as an entry vehicle into client systems to which the consultant would rarely have access using proactive methods.

The strength of Blocher's (1975) nine-step systematic eclectic interventionist model lies in its proactive nature and its applicability to virtually any organization. It is most helpful to trainees with its sophisticated and detailed entry process and the deliberate use of the sources of gain in psychology. Its major difficulty lies in its process orientation. This is a prime example of when an apprenticeship model of teaching consultation skills is needed, since focusing on processes of interaction is a demanding task.

Alinsky's (1972) advocacy consultation model in which the consultant focuses on helping powerless groups to obtain power through the selection and training of key indigenous leaders and through "behind the scenes strategizing" plays an important role in the training of consultants.

Since many students and trainees come from social classes which identify with the status quo and intact power groups, Alinsky's model helps to crystallize their class, sex and race biases. Along with having personal values jarred, the trainees exposed to Alinsky's values typically begin to perceive some of the boundaries of their thinking and start to play with new possible roles as a consultant. Ethical questions rarely raised in student services are addressed. For example, if a client system, say a department, refuses to give its workers "line" jobs, and never hires minorities or women, should a consultant accept a contract from the department? If the representatives of the staff, or minority and/or women faculty, ask the consultant to help them get hired or hired "on line" and all the "in house" channels are closed, how should a consultant act? Should, as Argyris (1970) suggests, consultants view themselves as professionals who will take on any clients (as, for example, when a civil liberties attorney represents the Ku Klux Klan in a free speech case)? Trainees are encouraged to consider to which subsection of this client system they feel the greatest allegiance and to speculate upon the impact of that identification on the consultation process.

The benefits of examining Alinsky's model lie in giving the trainees a novel consultation view, increasing their sense of what an appropriate client system can be, identifying their biases, and raising ethical issues.

The ecosocial model as described by Huebner (1977) provides trainees with a proactive model of consultation which simplifies diagnosis of system problems. The difficulty of the model for trainees is that the entry process often requires the consultant to be able to provide leadership for a team of high powered professionals (deans, department chairs, provosts) and that the data collection method requires experience and sophistication with building questionnaires and using standardized instruments. Giving trainees experience through the use of the apprenticeship model of consulting is imperative. In such an approach a senior consultant models the major facilitative roles and closely supervises the instrument development. The apprentice consultant can then participate at whatever level she/he is capable and comfortable.

Schein's (1969) process consultation model is presented to the class in the greatest depth since it is a difficult model and the concepts apply to all consultation cases. The process model can help a consultant working in a variety of different theoretical models to diagnose and understand system problems; it can also provide for the development of skills useful for the consultant's own work space.

One of the difficulties of this model is the trainees' lack of familiarity with either social psychology or with a wide variety of organizations. Trainees need to learn that understanding both process variables (communication networks, decision-making styles, problem-solving methods, cooperative versus competitive styles) and content variables (for instance, the distinction between schools, churches, and businesses) is central to being a competent, creative process consultant. One way to demonstrate this is to have trainees who are very familiar with one organization (high schools, churches, banks, campus police) critique the handling of a consultation case study by a colleague in class who is totally unfamiliar with the culture or the workings of that organization. From these experiences trainees learn both the kind of organization they prefer to work with and the kind of questions they need to ask of organizations with which they are unfamiliar.

As the trainees begin to master the various theoretical approaches to consultation, the focus of training should shift to applying these theories to appropriate situations. To help trainees find a systematic approach to applying consultation theory, an examination of the generic steps in consulting follows.

Generic Steps. The generic steps are those phases common to all consultation contracts if the consultant carries the client system to natural termination. These steps are: entry, contracting, planning, data collecting, intervention, evaluation, and termination. Although these phases are common to all consultation theories, they are often effected in very different ways. What follows is a brief discussion of some of the training issues present in these various steps.

The major difficulty in helping trainees to systematize their thinking about the various stages of consultation is a general lack of experience with each of the phases and an inability to assess the stage reached in any given phase, since consultation is very often a complex and nebulous process for the neophyte. For example, in the entry process the inexperienced consultant is usually struggling to demonstrate his or her expertise and may miss a lot of what is happening in the consultee system. The learning process can be facilitated if the trainees have practice in a safe setting to "see themselves" objectively without the threat that can exist in real life consulting.

A corollary task is to convince the trainees that each of these stages does exist and is important. For example, many trainees recoil at the notion of "diagnosing" a system or establishing a specific written contract. Many trainees are actually counselor trainees who have not yet learned to think of help-giving as sometimes involving the rather objective stance that a consultant may take. Thus it is important to discuss each of the stages in detail with the trainees and illustrate them, where possible, with examples from actual consultation interventions.

Issues in Consultation. Any training program should include an extensive discussion of some of the major issues for student services consultants. Values, ethics, the multiple roles of consultants, and the degree of one's knowledge of organizations are key issues, each of which is addressed in more detail below.

In some ways it seems terribly repetitive to discuss value issues in disciplines which deliver psychological services. Yet to ignore value issues would be a great omission, for to do so would be to ignore one of the more potent variables in the consultation. The value issue is two-sided. Consultants first need to determine whether they can agree with the client system's goals and feel professionally competent to help the client system reach them. The second side of the values question is the clarity of the consultants' values and their preferred mode of directiveness in the consulting process. In some of the consultation theories consultants are a highly active force in determining the direction of the consultation process (Alinsky; Caplan) while in others they are collaborative in goal formulations (ecosocial and Blocher).

Trainees can be sensitized to value issues by using role playing activities of initial contracting sessions. In the first round, the "client" states she wants, for example, an expert Caplan-styled consultant. Various trainees then take the role of the consultant contracting for services, but each plays a consultant from a different consultation model. In the second round, trainees act out client-consultant contracting sessions but neither tells which model they will operate out of. Observers then must determine which theoretical framework each trainee used and offer hypotheses concerning the success of the contracting.

The above situations outline covert ethical transactions. They are subtle since they have to do with the consultant's motivations and abilities. The more overt ethical transactions in consultation are well documented in both the *APA Monitor* (*Ethical Standards of Psychologists,* 1977) and the APGA Handbook on Ethical Guidelines (Callis, 1976) and do not need repetition here. Many of the ethical guidelines overlap with individual therapy practice (advertisement, soliciting business, double hats) and some are unique to consultation. Key ethical issues for the consultant coalesce around the multiple roles and relationships in which he or she is enmeshed, particularly in a complex system such as a university. For example, who is the client in a consultation involving residence hall vandalism: is it the resident life system or the staff of the particular hall, the students who live in the hall, or is it the client the vice president for student services who orders the consultation? What of the case in which a faculty member consults with a client who is a doctoral student of said faculty member?

It seems clear that the resolution of many of these issues depends on the role played by the consultant: external consultant, internal consultant, or change agent. Trainees should be sensitized to each of these roles: the external consultant with his inherent power; the internal consultant, often a prophet in his own land who competes with colleagues for power; the change agent, an advocate for the powerless. Trainees can only get a good "feel" for each of these roles by practicing them.

The knowledge of organizations is doubly important, providing for diagnostic ability in assessing client systems and familiarity with the real internal functioning of specific organizations. The diagnostic ability helps the trainees to boil down the information overload usually present in consultation work and helps to focus on the central issues. Familiarity with how a business or a hospital or a junior high school really works, and how the culture of these organizations operates, transforms trainees from foreigners who keep thumbing through their language guides to seasoned bilingual travelers. Real knowledge of an organization is hard to obtain without studying and working with it for years. Both diagnostic and cultural knowledge of organizations is so important that many consultants specialize by type of organization. Thus trainees must deal with their limitations as organizational consultants, despite the popularity of the notion of a "generalist" who can operate effectively in a number of different roles.

Consultation Skills. A course can only acquaint the trainee with the process skills needed by a consultant. For beginning professionals, additional training (supervised experience, working on consultation teams, and receiving feedback) is needed to acquire these skills. Communication and processing skills, application of the generic steps, instrumentation development, and designing and conducting of workshops are addressed in the class. For experienced professionals interested in inservice training less of this work will be necessary.

Most contracts are enhanced or diminished depending on the consultants' interpersonal communication skills. These are the same skills needed by individual therapists: warmth, empathy, positive regard, expression of feelings, abilty to accurately send and receive messages, establish trust, give and receive feedback, handle conflict, and accurately gauge client behavior. Development and use of these skills during the class and the laboratory experiences is encouraged.

Instrument development and data analysis constitute a separate category of skills since data collection makes up the backbone of the three models of consultation usually done on a college campus: action research; eco-mapping; and Blocher's systematic eclectic intervention model. Development of these skills often occurs while working with a skilled consultant in on-the-job training.

Given the enormous amount of course work already demanded in a doctoral program in counseling or psychology, advising students to take more course work in data collection methods seems idealistic. Huebner (1977) and Moore and Delworth (1976) suggest the creation of learning packets of specific skills which students or professionals could master as they became more interested in consultation work. Leonard (1977) observes that consultation expertise can be gained through an apprenticeship training model. These alternatives seem more viable for students than fifteen additional hours tacked onto a graduate program which may already represent 110 + credit hours. This assumes, however, that there are skilled consultants available for the apprentice and knowledgeable consultants to create learning packets on every campus. The alternative of no additional training presents serious ethical considerations for faculty and students and is unacceptable (Huebner and Banning, 1977).

Learning how to design and present workshops is an essential skill in consultation work, but one which is often ignored. Since the consultant often acts as a teacher and/or facilitator for a client system, the skills of determining behavioral goals, sequencing learning experiences, orchestrating didactic, practical and experiential material, and of designing the transfer of learning experiences are often overlooked. These skills can be learned through experiencing them as a trainee in consultation class and by having guided practice in designing and conducting workshops. Once again, doing consulting under supervision is one of the strongest ways of learning consultation skills. The experiential training section further illustrates this approach.

Practicum. Ideally, the practicum is built into the consultation class. The practicum begins with a review of various communication and process skills and moves to role playing the generic steps of consultation. It is followed with laboratory experiences in which the trainee both practices and leads the exercises. These laboratory experiences generally focus on teaching the participants to reflect on their own interpersonal and group behavior around such issues as trust, communication, and problem solving skills; cooperation and competition; power, race, sex and class bias, and general values clarification.

These experiences are followed by an exposure to terminated cases. The trainees are assigned to "rehash" the various consultation steps. Current cases are then examined in a case consultation format in which students can get a feel for the excitement and complexity of consultation work.

Trainees role play various theoretical approaches to entry, contracting, planning, intervention, evaluation and termination. "Impossible" consultation cases are examined and played with to stimulate trainees' thinking and daring. Afterwards, more typical examples of campus consultation cases are presented. The typical assignment here is to make suggestions for handling the case. If actual completed cases are discussed, the focus is on suggestions for change or improvement on the actions of the previous consultant. Current cases are then examined in a case consultation format in which trainees can gain experience vicariously for real consultation work. Consultants with various approaches who work on the campus (or other campuses) can be invited to discuss past cases or current work and challenge all parts of the trainer's and trainees' thinking and work.

Finally, a practicum experience should include either a team or an individual apprenticeship experience in an actual consultation case. It is important that plenty of time be built in for planning and debriefing. The major focus at this level of training is on selecting the aspect of the case the trainees can handle themselves and having appropriate supervision available.

Internship. An internship in consultation could be a traditional counseling internship with the additional focus and responsibilities of consultation clients, or a pre- or post-doctoral year experience concentrating solely on consultation work in a number of campus offices or departments.

An internship in consultation should provide for both a diversity of cases and some in-depth consultation experiences involving all phases from entry to termination. Depending on previous experience, interns usually begin working as team members with a senior consultant and move to assuming major responsibility for a contract under supervision. Interns are able to move in and work as co-consultant with an experienced consultant within the apprenticeship model if they have had a theory and practicum class in consultation. If they have not had these experiences, the supervisor needs to tailor intern involvement to tasks within the contract which the intern can handle. Background reading in consultation theory will be necessary for the intern to function as an apprentice.

Supervision. Some basic difficulties of consultation supervision include: not having enough interested or experienced staff, obtaining contracts and entries into systems to help the trainee begin, and enough time to be present at crucial decision points.

The preferred method of supervision in consultation is the apprenticeship model in which the trainee works either with and/or under a skilled consultant. If there are enough interns and supervisors, group supervision is an important additional mode which is enriching to all involved. It gives the trainees exposure to a wider variety of consultation experiences and issues than they individually could encounter. The trainees operate as a team of professionals addressing real problems, and see a variety of supervision and consultation styles.

The relationship between the supervisor and trainee is critical to the trainee's growth in consultation. Since the two will be in an apprenticeship relationship, the supervisor acts as the primary consultant on many of the projects and has firsthand information on the trainee's work. This allows the supervisor to make maximum use of modeling, reinforcement and successive approximations in developing the trainee. Multilevel value conflicts can be shared and discussed and the two persons can move over time from the apprenticeship model to a collaborative team model of doing consultation. Supervision of consultation should combine the presentation of didactic material with helping the trainee to confront his or her own strengths and weaknesses as a consultant. The manner in which the supervisor deals with integrating these areas will depend in large part on the experience level and openness of the trainee, as well as on the way in which the type of consultation model being used may interact with the trainee's personal style. Consultation supervision, like clinical supervision of counselors, demands a sensitive hand on the controls in order to maximize growth for the individual supervisee.

In-Service Training. Experienced staff may wish to develop or expand their consultation skills and not have a means of doing it. One of the difficulties in training experienced staff is determining which of their skills need improvement and, while recognizing their expertise in other arenas, providing them with sufficient supervision. An ongoing seminar is one way to help mature staff become acquainted with new theory and approaches without requiring that they take graduate courses. Coordinating staff development and obtaining learning packets which focus on consultation issues are some additional ways didactic material can be provided. A team approach seems to work best for maximizing in-service training, in which the experienced consultant "paddles stern" and guides the process while the inexperienced professional is right in the midst of the "white water."

summary

I have attempted to convey both the complexity and the potential involved in training consultants to work in a multi-level system such as a university. Consultation is a delicate, demanding, and delightful process which can help us to realize our goal of more efficient service delivery to the community. Trainees are faced with even more issues that require grappling with than are consultants, particularly since most trainees are at the lower levels of the system in terms of power and prestige. Helping trainees learn to navigate the shoals requires a number of environmental conditions and a relatively benign climate, as well as a thorough knowledge of and experience with various consultative models and strategies. Without this basis, there is no solidity or systematic effort. With such a grounding and with a favorable climate, the trip can be made with only minor hitches.

references

Alinsky, S. D. *Rules for Radicals.* New York: Random House, 1972.

American Psychological Association. *Ethical Standards of Psychologists.* Washington, D.C.: American Psychological Association, 1977.

Argyris, C. *Intervention Theory and Method: A Behavioral Science View.* Reading, Mass.: Addison-Wesley, 1970.

Bennis, W. C., and others (Eds.). *The Planning of Change* (3rd ed.) New York: Holt, Rinehart and Winston, 1976.

Bergin, A., and Garfield, S. (Eds.). *Handbook of Psychotherapy and Behavior Change.* New York: Wiley, 1971.

Blocher, D. H. "A Systematic Eclectic Interventional Model." In C. Parker (Ed.), *Psychological Consultation: Helping Teachers With Special Needs.* Reston, Va.: The Council for Exceptional Children, 1975.

Blocher, D. H. Personal Communication, 1973.

Brown, P. *Radical Psychology.* New York: Harper & Row, 1973.

Callis, R. (Ed.). *Ethical Standards Casebook.* Washington, D.C.: American Personnel and Guidance Association, 1976.

Caplan, G. *Principles of Preventive Psychiatry.* New York: Basic Books, 1964.

Drum, D., and Fiegler, H. "Achieving Total Outreach Potential: a Seven Dimension Model." *Impact,* 1973, *3* (2), 5-17.

Huebner, L. A. "Counseling Interventions: An Organizational-Interactional Approach." *The Counseling Psychologist,* 1977, *7* (2), 69-73.

Huebner, L. A., and Banning, J. H. *The Ethics of Intentional Campus Design.* Paper prepared for Division 17, Committee on Environmental Design in the College Campus Setting (R. K. Conyne, Chairman), 1977.

Leonard, M. M. "The Counseling Psychologist as an Organizational Consultant." *The Counseling Psychologist,* 1977, 7 (2), 73–77.

Leonard, M. M., and Collins, A. "Woman as Footnote." *The Counseling Psychologist,* forthcoming.

Moore, M., and Delworth, U. *Training Manual for Student Services Program Development.* Boulder, Col.: Western Interstate Commission for Higher Education, 1976.

Nutt, R. "Review and Preview of Attitudes and Values of Counselors of Women." *The Counseling Psychologist,* forthcoming.

Schein, E. *Process Consultation: Its Role in Organizational Development.* Reading, Mass.: Addison-Wesley, 1969.

Snow, D. L., and Newton, P. M. "Task, Social Structure, and Social Process in the Community Mental Health Center Movement." *American Psychologist,* 1976, 582–594.

*Mary M. Leonard is currently a senior staff psychologist
at the University of Maryland Counseling Center and
coordinator of the consultation team. She received her
training in consultation at the University of Minnesota under
the guidance of Dr. Margaret Hoopes and Dr. Donald Blocher.
Dr. Leonard also teaches a course in process
consultation and a practicum in campus consultation.*

Consultants are proactive change agents for others who should consider becoming proactive evaluators for themselves.

consultation evaluation: turning a circus into a performance

stephen c. paul

The systems theory perspective adopted in this volume creates the ideal backdrop for the following discussion of mediated service evaluation and accountability. Mediated service activities are defined in Chapter 5 as interventions which serve the ultimate recipient (individual or group) by impacting an individual or organization with whom the recipient interacts. Virtually all such activities involve consultation in some manner. In this chapter, the terms *mediated services* and *consultation* will be used as near-synonyms, with mediated services representing a broader category of all indirect interventions, thus including consultation but not restricted to consultation only. The intermediate individual or group will usually be referred to as the *consultee*. As defined, then, mediated services activities involve the interaction of one service system with another and, therefore, require a broader systems orientation. Evaluating and accounting for those involvements minimally requires a doubling of focus, to encompass the needs of both the agency offering service and the consultee agency.

evaluation

Definition. The basic aims of the evaluation process remain the same when considering a mediated intervention as when considering a direct intervention. Attkinsson and Broskowski (1978, p. 24) have comprehensively defined program evaluation as (1) a process of making reasonable judgments about program effort, efficiency, and adequacy which is (2) based on systematic data collection and analysis, is (3) designed for use in program management, external accountability, and future planning, and is (4) focused especially on accessibility, acceptability, awareness, availability, comprehensiveness, continuity, integration, and cost of services. Their definition explicitly identifies the general purposes, the nature of analysis, and the content areas of program evaluation. It helps us extend our thinking to accommodate the many aspects involved in thorough evaluation planning.

Weiss (1972) has pointed out that the major difference between research carried out for evaluative reasons and basic research is its purpose. Evaluative research is primarily intended to be used for decision making purposes. The Attkinsson and Broskowski (1978) definition suggests that evaluation supplies information concerning program effort, efficiency, and adequacy. That information can then be applied to program management, accountability, and planning decisions. The fact that evaluation research takes place in an action setting separates it from the pursuit of basic knowledge.

Measurement Validity. Measurement validity tells us whether we are actually measuring what we intend to measure. There are some very important validity issues in the evaluation of indirect or mediated services. One issue arises from the fact that indirect services are provided to intermediate consultees (for instance, resident hall advisors), who then directly influence the actual service recipients (e.g., students in the halls). The changes in the consultees (for instance, improved listening skills among the advisors) can be thought of as intermediate changes. Those changes in turn are expected to result in ultimate changes in the population of interest—the students. The consultant must keep in mind that the final criterion of intervention success is whether the students change, not the advisors. We monitor advisor changes to check on the intermediate goal; to ensure our ultimate goals, it is necessary to assess mediated service impact on the final intervention recipients as well (Cowen, 1978).

A second related issue is the timing of the consultant's measurements. This point applies to all measurements of program effectiveness. We very frequently are content to measure changes in intermediate or target groups immediately following the conclusion of our intervention efforts. Measurements conducted at that point only measure short-term program effects. The short-term gains may not endure. To be sure our interventions actually have the long-term effects we desire, later follow-up assessments should also be conducted (Weiss, 1972). Various ways to conduct such follow-up evaluations are discussed in an article by Reihman, Ciarlo, and Hargreaves (1977).

A third issue is that often the measures we can apply to mediated service evaluation are individually quite weak. For example, reports of program success or of satisfaction with a program from the perspective of the consultant, the consultee, or the service recipient are notoriously biased. The weakness of any single measure can be improved on by collecting converging measures (Cowen, 1978). Examples of direct measures include: interviews, questionnaires, psychometric tests, tests of information, interpretation, skills, and application of knowledge, projective tests, situational tests, diaries, and clinical examinations (Weiss, 1972). However, other indirect or unobtrusive measures can often economically supplement direct measurement techniques. Some readily available indirect sources of data include: observation, ratings by peers, staff, and experts, institutional records, available statistics, financial records, and other documents (Weiss, 1972). Most interventions are eventually intended to change some aspect of behavior; behavioral measures should therefore be included where feasible to add credibility to other types of measures. A discussion of the issues surrounding the selection of outcome measures for evaluating interventions can be found in Waskow (1975). Collecting multiple outcome measures will go a long way toward demonstrating whether or not changes are occurring as a result of an intervention.

A final issue is the question whether the planned intervention and the one actually delivered are one and the same. To be sure that they are, it is necessary to collect information about what actually occurs within the intervention. This measurement of process helps to explain why an intervention has the effects that it has. Weiss (1972) lists the following relevant process variables deserving measurement in an intervention: purpose, principles, methods, staffing, persons served, length of service, location, size of program, auspices, and management. We often worry about our outcomes without checking our inputs. Gathering process measures provides the assurance that you carried out the intervention which you thought you did.

Measurement Reliability. Measurement reliability indicates if our interventions have applicability to other times or settings. A mediated service intervention is a complex enterprise. Each intervention brings together a unique combination of persons, circumstances, and events. As a result it is very difficult to generalize from one intervention to another. Nevertheless, we often assume that a single report of a consultative intervention or a particular model provides guidelines for all similar interventions. We would think such conclusions regarding the evaluation of individual counseling activities quite foolish. The same reasoning applies to both instances. If we hope to extend our research conclusions beyond the setting in which they were gathered, we need to have information based on an adequate sample. This is not the case when we only have data on *one* mediated intervention. Cowen (1978) has commented that we will need replication of findings to gradually accumulate sufficient reliability concerning our interventions in community settings.

Organizational Issues. Organizational obstacles to the evaluation of intervention have received the attention of many writers (A Task Force of the Stanford Evaluation Consortium, 1976; Cowen, 1978; Perloff, 1976; Weiss, 1972). The following list represents a partial collection of problematic organizational factors: (1) the system complexity in terms of people, structures, and activities, (2) the constantly changing setting, (3) the haziness of program goals, (4) the political nature and wide variety of purposes, (5) the lack of motivation to engage in evaluation, (6) the costliness of evaluation in terms of time and money, (7) the lack of evaluation skills, (8) the infrequency of positive findings and the resulting threat to funding and personnel, (9) the differences in goals between the evaluator and organizational staff, and (10) the ubiquitous organizational resistance to change. This formidable array of deterrents suggests why many interveners hesitate to risk evaluating their pet project. Indeed, the track record of negative outcomes and/or disregarded outcomes strongly suggests that the apprehension may be well founded. With all of the confusion present in the organizational background, it is not too surprising that the comparative effects of a program may be hard to detect (A Task Force of the Stanford Evaluation Consortium, 1976).

Fortunately, the same writers who discuss the gloomy prospects for researching within an organization also offer some means of reducing some of the problems. The basic aim of all of their recommendations is the creation of an *environment* which will be receptive to various evaluation efforts. One procedure which reduces resistance to evaluation is to involve the administrators, managers, and staff of the organization in the planning of evaluation practices. The forming of a planning team composed of representatives of subgroups in the consultee agency at the outset of the intervention ensures adequate involvement (Moore and Delworth, 1976). Taking the time to give a thorough explanation of the purposes of the evaluation process can also reduce animosities. It is important to recognize that staff in the organization are likely to be more interested in the services delivered than in their evaluation. For that reason, it is wise to introduce as few and brief program disruptions as possible.

Other practices for eliminating organizational interferences deserve mention. It is worth the time invested to clarify the interveners' role in the consultee system and how they will relate to its authority structure. This will minimize unnecessary role ambiguity. Tensions regarding evaluation can be reduced further by reporting back useful information to those persons who can make use of it. Collected evaluative data will be more useful if they are presented in interpreted form with some concrete projections for future implications. Finally, the timing of data presentation is very important. Evaluation data should be collected in a way which corresponds with the organizational decision making process. Ill-timed reporting can defeat the purpose of an entire evaluation effort.

Lack of Precedent for Evaluation of Mediated Services. Barry (1970) reported a striking lack of literature on the evaluation of consultative activities. This situation has been remedied to some extent (Mannino, MacLennan, and Shore, 1975), but it is still difficult to trace articles on individual activities. Some of the reasons for the lack of published reports are self-evident. The previously noted infrequency of supportive findings plays a part. A second factor is the need felt by many agencies to consider evaluative research a personal property. Perhaps the best (and most optimistic) explanation is that much of evaluation research is used appropriately for internal program management purposes.

Some recent discouraging data concern evaluation and accountability of consultation/mediated services practices on college campuses (Hamilton, 1978a). Those data suggest that most university counseling centers do not evaluate their various consultative activities at all. It is also dismaying that most centers fail to keep accurate or complete records of their consultation/mediated services. These findings certainly offer one distressing explanation for the very limited reporting of consultation evaluation studies within the university community.

improving evaluation

Perkins (1977) has recently published an article which provides a framework for categorizing evaluative activities. The basic criterion for categorization is the intended purpose of the evaluation rather than the subject or method of evaluation. Perkins identifies six major purposes for which evaluation studies are carried out: (1) *Strategic* evaluation is typically conducted before a program begins in order to gather information on the establishment of organizational objectives (e.g., needs assessment). (2) *Compliance* evaluation is conducted to determine if the objectives of a particular program correspond with the established organizational objectives of the agency through which the program is delivered. (3) *Design logic* evaluations assess whether the assumptions which link the invested resources to program implementation, anticipated outcome, immediate outcome, and ultimate impact on the final problem are clear. (4) *Management* evaluations are intended to examine the effectiveness and efficiency with which agency resources are applied to achieve agency goals. (5) *Intervention effect* evaluations attempt to demonstrate the connection between the intervention activity and the outcome events. (Evaluations of the intervention process also fall into this category.) (6) The final type of evaluation designated by Perkins is the assessment of *program impact*. Program impact is concerned with whether or not the program attained its specified goals. An examination of the six distinct types of evaluation proposed by Perkins makes clear the fallacy of lumping evaluation activities into a single all-encompassing category. One must cautiously specify the purpose to be served by an evaluation before charging off into the sunset of data collection. Different types of data and data collection techniques would be appropriate, depending on the purposes.

Once the purpose of evaluations is specified, there is an impressive armamentarium of techniques for conducting them. These techniques include need assessment methods, experimental design, quasi-experimental design, pre-experimental design, goal attainment scaling, survey research, cost benefit analyses, cost effectiveness analyses, administrative audits, and operations research. There is much debate in the evaluation literature about which of these techniques is the "best" technique to apply to program evaluation. Each technique has its own proponents. But, as is often the case, we are disputing the wrong question. The appropriateness of the evaluation technique we employ is principally determined by the purpose for which we are evaluating. Weiss (1972) has pointed out that it makes little sense to carry out an intricate experimental design in situations where simple information gathering on some aspect of our intervention meets our aims better. With our purpose clear, we can proceed to select the most powerful method which can be applied within the restrictions of the situation. In evaluation, as in many other enterprises, the tools we use often come to be exaggerated far beyond the purposes for which they are employed.

The literature concerning the evaluative research on mediated activities is categorized on several other relevant dimensions as well. One dimension is the type of problem focused upon in the intervention (for example, vandalism). A second dimension specifies the type of system in which the intervention occurs (for instance, university residence halls). A third dimension might classify interventions on the basis of the level within the system at which it occurs (for example, administration). Other factors are conceivable. The array of mediated interventions described in the literature might be reported under any of these categories. They often are not designated consultative practices at all. As a result, any attempt to gather and compare the amorphous literature on "consultation" evaluation is far beyond the scope of this paper. The reader is referred to the bibliography of consultation studies to be found in Mannino, MacLennan, and Shore (1975) for representative studies. However, it is possible to abstract key principles which can be combined to form a working evaluation model for consultation/mediated services.

A Model of Consultation Evaluation. There seem to be certain commonly agreed upon stages which, with some variations, occur in the consultation process (Taylor, 1978; Watkins, 1976):

• Determination of the need for consultation.
• Initiation of the request for consultation.
• Organizational assessment and problem formulation.
• Mutual setting of objectives.
• Determination of strategies of action.
• Development of evaluation methods.
• Establishment of a working agreement.
• Implementation of action.
• Measurement and reporting of outcomes.

The planning of the evaluation of mediated services should be done early, prior to agreeing on the course of the intervention. Each mediated service intervention will vary in accordance with the nature of the organization in which it occurs, the level in the organization at which it is directed, and the type of problem addressed. The relevant evaluation practices will vary correspondingly. It is therefore impossible to propose one single consultation evaluation plan for all consultation practices; but it is possible to summarize the discussion up to this point by suggesting a general approach to expanding Stage 6 (Development of evaluation methods) into a model for planning consultation evaluation.

There are five basic steps to the model. *Step One* involves determining each purpose to be addressed by evaluative activities (e.g., management, intervention effect). There is very often more than one purpose which needs to be considered. As discussed earlier, it is this step which should guide the subsequent selection of the evaluation methods rather than the other way around.

Step Two involves determining the measurements which will be made. These measures will be selected as relevant indices of the intervention's objectives. Preferably, in all instances there will be measures which apply to both process and outcome aspects of the intervention. Process measures will include specifying the components and implementation of the delivered intervention itself (for instance, attendance at meetings). They might also point to what Weiss (1972) calls "bridging variables." For example, your intervention might increase a consultee group's awareness of available referral resources (bridging variable) which might subsequently influence the number of students using a new service on campus (outcome). Evaluating whether the group recalls the new referral sources could indicate whether the important bridging subgoal was attained.

Outcome measures most often are thought to refer solely to the intended effects of the intervention. In the previous example, a mediating outcome might be increased referrals made by the consultee group. The final outcome would be the increased use of the new service by the student population. However, it is equally important to measure unintended effects of intervention efforts. These unintended outcomes could be either positive or negative and may outweigh the intended outcomes. In the example above, a positive unexpected outcome may be that the awareness of referral sources reduces the number of instances where the consultee group handles problems outside its range of expertise. A possible negative effect might be to overload the new referral agency. Weiss (1972) has recommended that the evaluators should spend time "brainstorming" all of the possible consequences of their intervention.

Step Three follows directly from the intended purpose of the evaluation. In this step techniques of data collection appropriate to the purpose of the investigation are selected. The major goal here is to place the measures in a context which allows for their interpretation. One excellent schema for considering the connection among the purposes, criterion measures, and methodological tools of evaluation is presented by Attkinsson and Broskowski (1978, pp. 6-7). They have provided a table which breaks outcome purposes into categories of: (1) effort measurement, (2) performance measurement, (3) adequacy measurement, (4) efficiency measurement, and (5) process measurement. For each purpose, they list the typical criteria, informational requirements, and methodological tools, procedures, and indices. Their table provides a very helpful guide for consultants attempting to determine the components of their own evaluations.

Step Four of the evaluation process involves the planning of the actual collection of the measurements. Optimally, the measures will be gathered to reveal both short-term (immediately following the intervention) and long-term or follow-up effects. Returning to the referral example above, the enthusiasm of the consultant may result in contagion among consultees, leading to increased referrals immediately following the intervention. Once the consultant leaves the system, the use of referral sources may drop off dramatically. Short-term measures would not reveal this phenomenon; but with the additional long-term information, steps can be taken to build in necessary incentives to maintain the effects of the intervention.

Step Five is concerned with planning the manner in which the data gathered in the evaluation will be reported. This decision also depends on the purpose of the evaluation. Some of the purposes for which evaluation is conducted can be considered *formative* in nature: They are to be used to *build a program* which is being developed. All of the various types of purposes outlined by Perkins (1977) can be of a formative nature. Many people argue that this is in fact the major function of program evaluation. *Summative* evaluation research is typically concerned with what Perkins calls *program impact evaluations*. The data collected for this purpose are examined to determine whether an intervention achieves its intended goals and whether those are more efficiently or effectively met by this or other intervention approaches. Summative evaluations are often conducted for accountability reasons external to the intervention. Both formative and summative evaluation data should be reported to fit with decision making time schedules at levels appropriate to their purpose.

Consultants are in the unique position of being responsible to two possibly independent systems — the consultee system and their own. As a result, they need to collect evaluation information for each system. They may be establishing formative evaluation practices for the consultee system and summative research to justify their efforts in their own system. It helps to be aware that these two sources of evaluation needs exist. Problems could arise in the consultation relationship when the consultee system is unwilling to accept the evaluation needs of the consultant's system, or when the consultant subordinates the consultee system needs to his or her own. The best approach will make both sets of needs explicit and negotiate a satisfactory solution before the consultation is agreed upon.

Agency Benefits. Both the consultant and consultee agencies reap benefits from evaluation of mediated activities. It supplies a source of information which can greatly increase the range of questions which arise internally and externally to the intervention (Weiss, 1972). The summative type of evaluation can provide information for administrative decisions (deciding whether a program should be continued or discontinued). Summative evaluation may even help decide whether the underlying theory on which the intervention is based should be accepted or rejected. More frequently, formative evaluation contributes to internal decisions about intervention management. It can be incorporated into decisions about the allocation of resources and suggest modifications in the way the intervention is being carried out.

Program decisions are made regardless of whether evaluation data are available; even when they are, decisions are still based on political negotiations and administrative considerations (Weiss, 1972). Evaluation data can be valuable information to support those political stances. However, there are conditions under which such data contribute very little and evaluation may not be worth doing (Weiss, 1972): (1) when there are no questions regarding the program, (2) when the program's orientation is unclear, (3) when there is no agreement regarding its purpose, and (4) when there are insufficient resources in terms of staff training or funding to conduct the evaluation properly. Given the normal difficulties in evaluating services under the best conditions, evaluation under those circumstances is likely to result in failure. Perhaps the only condition worse than having no evaluation data at all is the situation where scarce resources are expended to conduct an uninterpretable evaluation.

accountability

Broskowski and Driscoll (1978), referring to human service programs, have commented that the whole concept of program evaluation must be viewed within the larger context of organizational structures and management. They make this point very strongly because the human service program is an open system, subject to continual internal change in response to a turbulent external environment. Unless service providers recognize this need to be aware of and responsive to these external changes, they will fail to maintain the viability of their own system.

It has been pointed out that one major function of evaluation is to provide information requested by decision makers to whom the consultants are responsible outside of their program. The external decision maker poses questions about service activities and the service provider responds with information, including evaluation data. The process of responding to those external information needs is termed *accountability*.

To Whom is the Consultant Accountable? Consultants tend to be very aware of the permeability of the boundaries of their system, since the nature of mediated services takes them outside their own agency on a regular basis. The range of persons to whom consultants become responsible multiplies by the number of other agency systems entered and by the very act of crossing over between what are typically horizontally administrated systems. To begin with they must justify the exit from their own agency and provide evidence of the value of the consultative activity over other types of work. This is often a difficult task in itself because the benefits to the consultant's own agency are often hard to measure. They may be a general reduction of problems within the larger, common university system; improved relations with a complementary agency; or other beneficial, but vague or remote outcomes. Secondly, consultants become accountable to the organization requesting their services. That agency or group will have needs of its own to document and justify the consultants' activities. Thirdly, consultants have the additional responsibility to ensure that the intervention they introduce into the consultee system has its own accounting practices to ensure responsiveness to the consultant system.

Accountability as I have been describing it so far can be thought of as a reactive process. Typically the external request for information is initiated and the agency responds. The common sources of requests for reactive accountability information are administrators, funders, and members of the agency staff. Recently service consumers themselves have begun to request documentation of program effectiveness and efficiency. Many times service agencies are accountable to accrediting committees comprised of a group of their professional peers who monitor their activities as well.

Service accountability can also be initiated on a proactive basis. The service provider can initiate reporting prior to an externally expressed need for information. There are some clear advantages to proactive reporting, particularly for the mediated service providers (both for their own activities and those of the intervention recipient). As a political move, submitting information shows a willingness to be responsive to the external system—certainly a welcome change for most administrators. A second political gain would be the permission to set up the nature and method of reporting. It is often hard to force mediated services into categories developed by persons unfamiliar with them. Such distortions could produce the appearance of ineffectiveness, which may be due to the irrelevancy of the requested information rather than to a lack of accomplishments. Setting up appropriate reporting systems sidesteps this risk. By building accountability rationale and procedures directly into the program from the outset, it is possible to avoid the "evaluation syndrome" which arises from a resistance to externally imposed, reactive accountability demands. Consultant reporting can also be a means of raising the level of understanding of your activities. Moore and Delworth (1976) have commented that reporting directed toward students and others—faculty, for instance—in addition to administrators can result in increased support for activities.

Does Accountability Interfere? Heavy demands placed on a program for reactive reporting for which it does not have resources can be a burden. Responding to the requests requires a redirection of the consultant's service aims. As noted earlier, evaluation conducted without sufficient resources is unlikely to meet its purposes. The end result is a frustrated effort and unsatisfactory reporting. Over-emphasis on outcome evaluation could divert resources from more pressing needs for formative research which could guide program development. It is important to meet with those who make an accountability request to make sure that both they and the consultants have a clear understanding of the purpose of the reporting. By clarifying the purpose, it is possible to cooperate in finding a method which serves both needs. The purpose of the desired accountability procedures should guide the reporting, just as the purpose should guide the selection of an evaluation method. At least a discussion of the purpose can help consultants to resign themselves to the need for the type of accounting requested.

The best way to avoid the trap of unpreparedness for a request for information is to develop a well thought out and comprehensive management information system (MIS). The information system attends to the wide range of differing purposes for which information is essential. An MIS routinely answers the following questions (Sorenson and Elpers, 1978): (1) What services are provided and to whom? (2) What resources are being used to deliver those services? (3) How effectively are the aims of the service being met? (4) How efficiently are the resources of the service being used to supply the services? Once an MIS has been perfected, the requests of administrators, funders, consumers, and others can be met by organizing readily available data into a report which meets their special needs. An added benefit is the ability to conduct planning and management control of internal resources from the same central data process. Consultants should plan to fit into the MIS of the consultant and consultee agencies. Where no MIS exists, it would still be wise to build an MIS for internal purposes. For a thorough discussion of the implementation of an MIS see Sorenson and Elpers (1978).

Organizational Issues. Many of the same organizational constraints presented with regard to evaluation also pertain to the issue of accountability. However, there are several special accountability issues which arise for consultant roles in their own agency. There is often a discrepancy between the commitment which members of an agency verbalize and the actual support provided for consultative activities. In reality, hours invested in mediated services are often implicitly thought of as "stolen" from direct service provision. There are often no clearly worked out agency priorities indicating the relative value of the invested time and resources. As the survey of counseling centers revealed, there is generally no conceptualization guiding consultative functions. Similarly there is seldom any clear way of reporting mediated interventions or integrating them with direct service efforts. In the past the lack of specification of consultative activities may have avoided confrontations regarding agency priorities; but the time has come when agencies, and not just particular services, must justify themselves. With that shift, *all* of the output of an agency, including its previously unreported mediated activities, must be clearly specified and accounted for.

There are also certain unique issues which arise in the consultee organization. One issue has to do with the consultant's alien status in the consultee group. Quite understandably, there may be some concerns regarding the maintenance of confidentiality by the consultant. This is especially a concern when the consultant agency (for instance, counseling center) and consultee agency (residence halls) are both situated within the same administrative structure (student services). A second issue pertains to the notions of role status and territoriality. A consultant who enters a sister agency professing superior status and expertise and disparaging in act or word the competence of the members of that organization quickly antagonizes the consultee group. It is extremely important that the consultant acknowledge the expertise of the consultee group and show due respect. Crossing between organizations and disciplines often aggravates already existing guild and competence concerns.

Improving Mediated Service Accountability. It is increasingly critical that mediated activities be adequately represented to administrators. There are currently several basic reasons why they are not. The first of these reasons is that agencies are only beginning to acknowledge the integral value of their mediated service programs. This may be a reflection of national trends toward mediated activities as well as administrative demands to serve more of the consumer population's needs. The second reason is that the term "consultation" has deceptively suggested an oversimplified view of the wide range of activities conducted in a mediated way, interfering with understanding and reporting. Third, the types of activities that mediated service interveners carry out have not been easily accommodated into the agency MIS which has been built with direct services in mind. Last, we are still struggling with ways to understand and evaluate mediated service offerings.

To alleviate the reporting confusion, it has been necessary to come up with a framework of categories which adequately depict the variety of mediated activities. One such framework has been drawn from a scheme developed by Caplan (1964). Modifications of this framework have been employed in community mental health centers (Bietel and Levenson, 1978) and counseling centers (Hamilton, 1978b). Basically, the framework divides consultation activities into nine categories of methodologies: (1) client-centered case consultation, (2) consultee-centered consultation, (3) program-centered administrative consultation, (4) consultee-centered administrative consultation, (5) staff training/education, (6) workshop, (7) demonstration, (8) lecture, (9) other. Mediated service activities are assigned to a category on the basis of the focus and type of intervention provided.

The framework allows mediated activities to be recorded in a record keeping system on an ongoing basis. Ideally, this system will fit directly into other ongoing agency recording procedures. At the Colorado State University Counseling Center (Hamilton, 1978b), this has been successfully accomplished for consultant reporting to the consultant agency. Folders which are kept on consultation activities correspond with the folders kept on direct service contacts. They contain a consultation intake form which records data on the consultee organization, the problem, recommendations concerning the type of consultation indicated, and suggested disposition. A process summary form calls for a problem definition, description of the intervention process, documents collected (for example, a contract), a statement of extent of fulfillment of the working contract, and a prognosis for the future maintenance of program effects. The consultee group is asked to complete a mediated service evaluation form on which they rate aspects of the consultation process. Finally, the mediated service client folder contains a closing summary form which sums up the consultant-consultee interaction throughout the intervention. This basic reporting procedure supplies the same type of information on mediated service interventions as is collected on direct interventions, making comparisons feasible.

In order to provide the information necessary to monitor the extent and type of mediated service activity and allocate resources, a second type of reporting system is necessary. That system monitors the activities of the individual service providers. The format developed at Colorado State University requires the individual to report mediated service activities as part of a daily time log along with other types of activities engaged in.

Theodore Lownik Library
Illinois Benedictine College
Lisle, Illinois 60532

An alternative individual activity reporting system (Beigel and Levenson, 1978) was developed at the Southern Arizona Community Mental Health Center (SACMHC). The SACMHC report is based upon the same basic Caplan model. However, this report is compiled on a weekly basis rather than a daily basis. This may be a more expedient method of reporting mediated services in a system where no daily log is kept.

The consultant is faced with accountability responsibilities in the consultee agency as well. There are two basic ways in which accountability within the consultee system must be attended to. In the first place, the consultant must evaluate the entire consultation process and its outcome with the consultee in light of the stipulated contract which they originally agreed upon. Secondarily, consultants will probably want to build accountability practices into activity which they initiated. If they accomplish these two ends in the consultee system, they will leave that system with the assurance that the consultee's needs have been met and that the intervention impact will continue to be assessed.

summary

This chapter has attempted to describe the special practices and concerns which apply to evaluation and accountability in mediated services. The two activities are very closely related as they pertain to program management, external accountability, and program planning. A number of issues have been raised which offer potential obstacles to the development of sound evaluation and reporting practices. However, a number of ways to reduce the seriousness of those obstacles have also been presented. Additionally, suggestions for constructing mediated service evaluation and accountability practices have been offered. The chapter ultimately has tried to depict the complex roles that consultants must assume as they navigate between both the consultant and consultee systems.

references

A Task Force of the Stanford Evaluation Consortium. "Evaluating the Handbook of Evaluation Research." In G. V. Glass (Ed.), *Evaluation Studies Review Annual*, 1976, *1*, 195–215.

Attkinsson, C. C, and Broskowski, A. "Evaluation and the Emerging Human Service Concept." In C. C. Attkinsson and others (Eds.), *Evaluation of Human Service Programs*. New York: Academic Press, 1978.

Barry, J. R. "Criteria in the Evaluation of Consultation." *Professional Psychology*, 1970, *1*, 363–366.

Beigel, A., and Levenson, A. I. "Program Evaluation on a Shoestring Budget." In C. C. Attkinsson and others (Eds.), *Evaluation of Human Service Programs*. New York: Academic Press, 1978.

Broskowski, A., and Driscoll, J. "The Organizational Context of Program Evaluation." In C. C. Attkinsson and others (Eds.), *Evaluation of Human Services Programs*. New York: Academic Press, 1978.

Caplan, G. *Principles of Preventive Psychiatry*. New York: Basic Books, 1964.

Cowen, E. "Some Problems in Community Program Evaluation Research." *Journal of Consulting and Clinical Psychology*, 1978, *46*, 792-805.

Hamilton, M. K. "Survey of Consultation Activities in College Counseling Centers." Fort Collins: University Counseling Center, Colorado State University, 1978.

Hamilton, M. K. Personal Communication, 1978b. (Colorado State University's Counseling Center has created a record system for evaluation and accountability purposes; no published materials describing the system exist.)

Mannino, F. V., MacLennan, B. W., and Shore, M. F. (Eds.). *The Practice of Mental Health Consultation.* New York: Gardner Press, 1975.

Moore, M., and Delworth, U. *Training Manual for Student Service Program Development.* Boulder, Colo.: Western Interstate Commission for Higher Education, 1976.

Perkins, N. T. "Evaluating Social Interventions: A Conceptual Schema." *Evaluation Quarterly*, 1977, *1*, 639-656.

Perloff, R., Perloff, E., and Sussna, E. "Program Evaluation." *Annual Review of Psychology*, 1976, *27*, 569-594.

Reihman, J., Ciarlo, J. A., and Hargreaves, W. A. "A Method for Obtaining Follow-up Outcome Data." In W. A. Hargreaves, C. C. Attkinsson, and J. E. Sorenson (Eds.), *Resource Materials for Community Mental Health Program Evaluation.* (2nd ed.) DHEW Publication Number ADM 77-328. Washington, D.C.: U.S. Government Printing Office, 1977.

Sorenson, S. E., and Elpers, J. R. "Developing Information Systems for Human Service Organizations." In C. C. Attkinsson and others (Eds.), *Evaluation of Human Service Programs.* New York: Academic Press, 1978.

Taylor, E. N., and Vineberg, R. "Evaluations of Indirect Services to Schools." In C. C. Attkinsson and others (Eds.), *Evaluation of Human Service Programs.* New York: Academic Press, 1978.

Waskow, I. E. "Fantasied Dialogue With a Researcher." In I. E. Waskow and M. B. Parloff (Eds.), *Psychotherapy Change Measures.* DHEW Publication Number ADM 74-120. Washington, D.C.: U.S. Government Printing Office, 1975.

Watkins, E. L., Holland, T. P., and Ritho, R. A. "Improving the Effectiveness of Program Consultation." *Social Work in Health*, 1976, *2*, 43-54.

Weiss, C. H. *Evaluation Research: Methods of Assessing Program Effectiveness.* Englewood Cliffs, N.J.: Prentice-Hall, 1972.

*Stephen C. Paul is currently a staff psychologist in the
University of Utah Counseling Center. He has been involved
in mediated services delivery at all levels of university systems.
He participated in consultation activities during graduate
training at the University of Missouri-Columbia,
and internship training at Colorado State University.*

Administrators wishing to consult for institutional change
must be able to negotiate political and ethical quagmires
or risk seeing their goals (and themselves) slowly sinking.

consultation for environmental change: an administrator's view

james h. banning

Consultation for environmental or institutional change is a *political* process. (The term *political* as used here refers to any process or event which affects governmental or administrative functioning. Particular dynamics or conflicts might be expected to exist or occur as part of that process or event.) Like all political processes within an institutional setting, consultation can be a powerful activity as well as a hazardous one. The student services administrator who plans to use the consultation process to bring about institutional change should be familiar with the issues involved in such activity: the political nature of consultation, the importance of an ecological perspective for student services administrators, understanding of and guidelines for institutional change, associated professional and political issues, and finally, questions of participation. These topics are of critical importance for administrators who plan to use consultation for change within the institutions they serve.

consultation and student services administration

The process described by the term consultation no doubt extends farther back into the history of human services delivery than the formal concept itself. This also is true within the specific system of student services. Particular theories and models of consultation are described in Chapter 1. There are some generic characteristics of consultation which make it an especially appropriate tool for student services administrators and staff.

Key components of the consultation process (pre-entry, entry, gathering information, defining the problem, determination of the problem solution, stating objectives, implementation of plan, evaluation, and termination) have been described (Kurpius, 1978). Most or all of these components are found in the routine activities of student services administrators as they work with various systems on the campus. Conceptualizing group or organizational interventions within the framework of the consultation process gives a useful structure for administrative planning and evaluating of individual parts of the consultative relationship. For example, a new administrator might see his/her efforts to quickly contact and meet key personel around campus as part of a general stage of pre-entry; that is, establishing relationships to facilitate later entry into systems when immediate needs arise.

The flexibility of the consultative mode is demonstrated by the fact that consultation has occurred in a wide variety of settings; for example, in schools, medical and social service agencies, business organizations, religious organizations, governmental agencies, justice agencies, and community organizations. Parallel organizations are found on most campuses, and administrators may productively use the experiences of consultants in nonacademic communities to gain insight about counseling with the widely varied subsystems on campus.

Finally, as Lippitt and Lippitt (1977) point out, the consultant may take many roles: advocate, technical specialist, trainee/educator, collaborator in problem-solving, alternative identifier, fact finder, process specialist, and reflector. Administrators frequently use such roles.

Background. The advent of the student development model for student services (Parker and Morrill, 1974; O'Bannion and Thurstone, 1972) and the increasing complexity of higher education have contributed to recent statements supporting the appropriateness of consultation as an appropriate strategy for student services administrators and staff (Miller and Prince, 1976). Another key development is the increasing demand for student services staff to serve as consumer advocates for students; this is in response to the general consumer movement of the last two decades (Bevilacqua, 1976). A trend toward attempting to affect as many individuals as possible, to have maximum impact on the campus, has also created a greater willingness among student services staff to be involved in consultation (McGehearty, 1968).

University counseling centers are probably the student services component most analyzed for involvement in consultation. In a 1971 survey of 71 counseling centers in the Western states, 78.9 percent of the centers reported they were involved in consultation within the university setting and 43.7 percent reported being involved in consultation outside the university. The amount of staff time allocated to consultation activity, however, was reported to be less than ten percent (Banning and Aulepp, 1971). A survey of the outreach practices of counseling centers across the country in 1975 indicated that eleven percent of the 220 reported outreach programs involved field and community consultation (Morrill and Banning, 1973).

More general involvement of student services staff in consultation has also been studied. A survey of student services administrators at 200 colleges and universities attempted to analyze their divisions' degree of involvement in a consultant role. The investigation revealed a high degree of involvement in specific kinds of consultation, particularly in extracurricular components of the campus, and in increasing the amount of research about student life. Respondents reported varied amounts of perceived administrative support for consultation. The author suggested examples of potentially fruitful consultative interventions, and proposed the consultant role as a way of synthesizing efforts and roles for student services workers (Pyron, 1974).

Environmental/institutional change. The field of student personnel administration has begun to include within its scope the notion of environmental or institutional change (Harvey, 1974). There is growing support for restructuring campus environments to foster a sense of community (Tollefson, 1975). The use of consultation to assist in bringing about institutional change presents some substantial challenges and political issues. One major issue is the fact that student services administrators, using consultation, historically have been involved (perhaps unknowingly) in the process of maintaining the *status quo* and not in institutional change. Altrocchi, (1972 p. 506), observed that consultation "is usually oriented more toward conserving rather than changing the *status quo* of the consultee's institutions and of society." This observation is further endorsed by Blake and Mouton (1976) in their discussion of strategies of consultation. They point out that two types of consultation intervention strategies most often support the *status quo*. They state that "the acceptant approach of emotional barrier-reduction and the catalytic approach of helping people to make progress in dealing with given situations are most likely to aid individuals and groups to do a better job within the existing 'status quo' " (Blake and Mouton, 1976, p. 65). Whether or not campus consultation primarily serves as an instrument of change or as a protector of the *status quo* depends upon the perspective or the political stance of the student services administrators who plans to employ the consultation process.

an ecological perspective for student services administrators

The historical perspectives that have guided the student services administrator have been more protective of the *status quo* than supportive of institutional change (Banning and Kaiser, 1974), probably because many student services administrators have assumed a position in which primary attention has been given to encouraging individual students to adjust to existing conditions. An alternative is attempting to adjust existing campus conditions to be more responsive to the ever changing developmental needs of students and to the fluctuating nature of the student population; this is the ecological or institutional change approach.

No doubt the philosophy of *in loco parentis* was at one time a reasonable response to the developmental status of college students. But the concept was retained for too long after it had failed to respond to the changing developmental needs of students. Much activity in student services was focused on how to get students to "fit" the *in loco parentis* model rather than in designing a new model or perspective that would better fit the needs of students.

The same pattern can be seen in the relationship between various "new" or nontraditional populations on campuses and the institutions' response. The past and perhaps all too often the continuing approach has been to require ethnic minorities, adult students, and students with disabilities to adjust to the campus environment as it is. It has only been with the pressure from federal legislation (Title VI, Title IX, and the "504" Regulations) that institutions of higher education have begun to change in order to be more responsive to the needs of the new groups on campus.

By assuming the goal of helping individual students adjust to the existing educational environment without evaluating it, the student services administrator is promoting the maintenance of the *status quo*. Despite the good intentions indicated by the goal of helping students to adjust and develop, the traditional perspective may, in fact, contribute to the survival of a destructive or non-growth-inducing environment.

An ecological position balances the onesidedness of the traditional position. The essence of the ecological perspective is in understanding and affecting the transaction between students and their environment. The ecological position therefore encompasses the influence of the institution on the students and *vice versa*. From this perspective both students and administrators have joint responsibility for changing the institution/student interface to produce the optimal educational/growth-inducing environment. Only by accepting this responsibility can the student services administrator gain credibility as someone with the potential to deliver consultation that will create desirable institutional change. Unless he or she adopts the ecological perspective, the administrator's consultation activity may be suspected of merely promoting adjustment on the part of those oriented toward changing the institution. For example, a group of residence hall students may have started a food fight to highlight the poor quality of food. A *status quo* intervention might include consultation leading to greater supervision of the dining room and/or severe penalties for the disruptive behavior. Even if the demands for better food were recognized and meals were changed accordingly, this still could be a *status quo* intervention. If, on the other hand, the intervention strategy led to students' being involved on a routine basis in the discussion/decision process of menu preparation, then significant institutional change would have occurred. The latter change allows for the menu preparation process to respond to changing needs of students. As in most institutional changes involving a participatory component, the change also allows for an educational experience (learning about the problems and techniques associated with institutional food services). Our consultations should, like this one, lead to better fit between students and their environment.

understanding institutional change

Before consultation can become a viable part of an institutional change strategy, some understanding or model of the change process is necessary. One model is offered by Martorana and Kuhns (1975). They propose an interactive theory for change in higher education. As viewed by these authors, change comes about through interaction of personal, extrapersonal, and goal hiatus forces. Personal forces may be persons of three kinds: decision makers, implementors, and consumers. Decision makers are influential persons in the institution such as the president, academic administrators, board members, or such bodies as the faculty senate. Implementors are those on campus who carry out the decisions. Consumers are the students, alumni, parents, legislators and, at times, citizens at large.

Extrapersonal forces are of two kinds, tangible and untangible. Tangible influences on institutional change include such factors as facilities, equipment, and available monies. Intangible influences include such variables as policies, traditions, and laws.

The third force for change is called goal hiatus, which refers to the discrepancy between the aspiration toward a particular institutional goal and the achievement of that goal. Change comes about as the result of the interaction of these three forces: personal, extrapersonal and goal hiatus. For example, at times change occurs because of the charisma of an individual policy maker (a personal force); the influence of federal legislation (an extrapersonal force) may also be a help or a hindrance. At times the sense of disappointment within the institution regarding failure to reach a goal (goal hiatus) may cause change. Any one of these forces or their interactions may bring about the accomplishment of a goal.

If institutional change is the result of these interactive forces, what specific change strategies are available to affect them? Martorana and Kuhns (1975) define a strategy as an overall plan of action for achieving a particular goal. A strategy for campus change is an overall design used to move the institution toward a goal. These authors go on to identify the following strategies: low-profile action, systematic experimentation, participant involvement *versus* power coercion, creation of demand, development of legitimacy, creation of power blocs, control of internal organization, and control of communications. They also speak to the topic of tactics. Tactics are described as specific actions taken to accomplish a particular strategy. The following are examples of tactics: appreciation of timing, obtaining an overview, determining obstacles, providing reassurance, building on existing concerns, avoiding rejection, respecting the past, persuading the opposition, confronting the opposition, compromise and co-opting, selecting personnel for decision making positions, using trial balloons, using a front man, carrying out a hidden agenda, and outflanking the opposition.

The authors point out that tactics and strategies may have both positive and negative connotations. As a result, certain tactics and strategies are less desirable at times because of ethical and political considerations. These ethical or political concerns, coupled with the complexity of the change process, call for common sense guidelines for administrators who want to use the consultation process to bring about institutional change.

Guidelines for the adminstrator. For the ecologically-oriented administrator who plans to use consultation as a tool, certain operating assumptions are useful to aid in that political undertaking. Shepard (1972) has discussed a number of ideas that can be transformed into a set of guidelines for administrators. The first is "stay alive." The politics involved in working with an entire campus system can create situations in which the survival of an administrator can be jeopardized. Keeping in mind the need to "stay alive" helps prevent self-sacrifice on behalf of a cause that you do not wish to be your last. This is not to say that risks should not be taken, but that they should be taken only after careful study. It is easy to die for a cause, more difficult to live for one. Of particular importance in "staying alive" in an institution of higher education is allowing factual data to talk for you. Solid research data highlighting the need for and the direction of the desired institutional change are extremely difficult to combat; this is in contrast to a personal opinion or philosophy that may point in the same direction. For example, the strategy of producing data showing how many lives are disrupted on campus due to unwanted pregnancy may be more useful in establishing a birth control clinic than merely promoting the philosophy that women should control their own bodies.

To "start where the institution is" serves as a second guideline. This requires good assessment techniques. Often interventions fail because they are not empathic with the system. They are often too abrasive or threatening. Obviously the best initial attempt to make an unresponsive institution more responsive to the health needs of its women students may not be the promotion of an abortion clinic. The overriding goal is moving the institution toward the desired ultimate change, not testing how fast you can move while endangering the entire goal.

A third guideline is to "ride the surf." Within an institution there are often natural happenings that have their own momentum. This suggests that you are more likely to successfully implement a change if that change coincides with the natural momentum ("surf") in the environment. It is often easier to direct existing energies than to create them. Recent "surfs" in higher education, for example, have been associated with federal legislation regarding ethnic minorities, women, and students with disabilities. The impetus given by federal legislation can be directed into desirable, substantial institutional change.

"Don't use one when two could do it" is a fourth guideline for administrators involved in institutional change. Do not try to bring about change single-handedly when a team effort is possible. Not only may better ideas and strategies emerge through a team effort; it is also harder to destroy or sabotage a team than an individual change agent. If you have others involved with you, it helps to counteract your assuming the "hero" role and the high probability of self-sacrifice. If you are pushing to overthrow outdated student health policies for women students, it is helpful to have support from concerned women students and from the local medical association as well. The building of power blocs can be helpful.

A final guideline is "don't argue if you can't win." If it looks like your proposed intervention will receive an institutional "no," back off and come back later. "No's" must be turned into "yes's" in order to succeed. Often people defend their original positions more strongly the more they are pressured; *always* try to avoid "no" responses.

Useful models of institutional change are available. Guidelines exist to help master the political process of consultation for institutional change. However, several significant political and ethical issues remain to be discussed.

environmental change: professional and ethical issues

Administratively assisting individuals, groups, and organizations to bring about campus change certainly requires competent consultation. Most definitions of consultation are relevant to this process. The stages of consultation appear to have applicability, and the various roles consultants may assume may be useful ones for the administrator. Some key professional and ethical issues, however, present challenges to the administrator. Such issues are always present at the interface between consultant and institution. As outlined by Conyne, Banning, and others (1977) and Pfeiffer and Jones (1977), these interface issues include questions of advocacy, competency, value systems and organizational issues. All are interrelated; but a brief description of each will again highlight the complexity of consulting for institutional change from an administrative position.

In the past ten years the advocacy movement has increasingly influenced campus administration. Professionals of all kinds have become involved in responding to the needs of various groups of disadvantaged clients or clients who are members of unique groups or classes with special needs (Argyris and Schon, 1974); certainly students services professionals have been strongly affected by such advocacy issues as student rights in general, issues of due process, and others (Bevilacqua, 1976). Advocacy questions produce particularly complex problems for student services administrators with a commitment to institutional change. For example, administrators might be strongly committed to increasing services for returning students who have special needs because of the fact that most campus services have been planned for students of traditional ages. They make deliberate attempts to change the environment to assist the returning students, and problems ensue. Other staff might question the goals of the intervention and might wonder whether the administrator has the right to make unilateral or personal decisions about priorities for the entire campus. Other groups might complain about a relative lack of attention to *their* special needs. The administrator might find that the goals of the institution are not congruent with his or her goals for these services, or that the agency asked to supply the services is unwilling to do so because of its pre-established goals. Deciding which, if any, groups to actively support is an ethical issue for an administrator, and the process of giving that support is fraught with political problems. Administrators face similar problems when members of their staffs or agencies within their divisions engage in advocacy for a particular group. If a university student relations office decided to make returning students a high-priority target population, the administrator might choose to actively support the agency, to attempt to remain neutral, or to dissuade the agency from its plan. In any advocacy case, administrators must use consultation skills to respond to the often conflicting opinions of the many campus subsystems which might be affected.

Competence is of critical importance. In one investigation (Shore and Golann, 1969) the question was raised whether psychologists were competent at all to take on community work without being retrained. The question is equally relevant for counselors or college student personnel workers using consultation as a tactic for institutional change. Most graduate programs do not offer students classroom or practicum experiences in consultation. When they do, they often encompass only a traditional approach involving mental health consultation. Similarly, the topic of environmental or institutional change is unlikely to be a part of the student's program. The problem here is that while institutional intervention may become the "treatment of choice" for environments, the training to carry out such treatment is sorely lacking.

One of the more troublesome issues is that of values. The value issue affects the very core of all intervention strategies. Two basic approaches to the problem of values are apparent (Conyne and others, 1977). One is to claim a value-free position. In this case, the consultant would bring skills and knowledge to a system, but would allow the host organization or institution to choose which values and goals to pursue. This position allows the consultant to function as a "non-directive" institutional consultant. Maintaining this position, however, does not lead to neutrality. Consultants to organizations almost by definition find themselves serving the organization that arranged for their services. Would an organization allow a consultant to disrupt its very existence? In reality, I believe, the position of value-free consultation is untenable, particularly in the area of institutional change.

The second approach suggested by Conyne and others (1977) would be to become aware of one's own values and to use this knowledge within the consultation process. This position may lead, however, to the imposition of one's own values upon the institution. At some point in any consultation an institutional consultant will almost inevitably have to define his or her values and to assess (as an ethical responsibility) whether they are congruent enough with the organization's to allow him or her to continue — or initiate — the consultation. A common example of an incongruence is relevant to earlier discussion; often a consultant may have a basically institutional-change orientation and be asked to work within a *status quo*-oriented campus. Perhaps one workable solution is an open discussion between the consultant and the institution regarding the values of each. Such discussion would demand a level of trust so that differences could be monitored and worked on throughout the relation-ship.

Organizational issues also require constant consideration. How much of an agency's time should be spent in consulting for institutional change as opposed to offering direct client services? How much time should the student services administrator spend in trying to change the institution? How can an agency or an administrator offer consultation to the organization of which they, in fact, are a part? Motives of the agency or the administrator may be frequently questioned. A high level of sophistication on the part of the admin-istrator is required to allow ongoing monitoring of these questions.

the participatory perspective

Given the complexity of the process of consultation for institutional change and the many political, professional, and ethical issues such activity raises, there is a need for a basic perspective to guide the consultant. Building on the work of those interested in environmental interventions, I believe the participatory perspective provides the most reasonable way to proceed. This perspective calls for the active involvement of all (or the largest possible num-ber of) members of the institution that will be affected by the consultation effort. This perspective maintains that institutional change activities must include participation by all who would be affected in order for the activities to be ethically sound. Adherence to this perspective should work against the pos-sibility of a select few (such as the consultant) controlling the behavior of many. The foregoing issues and questions surrounding advocacy, values, and organizational concerns become somewhat more manageable using this parti-cipatory framework. Implementation of this perspective on the level of repre-sentation and the mechanics of reaching a reasonable consensus can be extremely difficult. However, the perspective, if successfully achieved, pro-vides resolution to some very complex ethical and political problems.

references

Altrocchi, J. "Mental Health Consultation." In S. E. Golann and C. E. Eisdorfer (Eds.), *Handbook of Community Mental Health,* New York: Appleton-Century-Crofts, 1972.

Argyris, C., and Schon, D. A. *Theory in Practice: Increasing Professional Effective-ness.* San Francisco: Jossey-Bass, 1974.

Banning, J. H., and Aulepp, L. A. *Program Activities and Student Utilization of Campus Mental Health Facilities in the West.* Western Interstate Commission for Higher Education, Monograph 3. Boulder, Col., 1971.

Banning, J. H., and Kaiser, L. "An Ecological Perspective and Model for Campus Design." *Personnel and Guidance Journal,* 1974, *52,* 370-375.

Bevilacqua, J. P. "The Changing Relationship Between the University and the Stu-dent: Implications for the Classroom and Student Personnel Work." *Journal of Col-lege Student Personnel,* 1976, *17* (6), 489-494.

Blake, R. R., and Mouton, J. S. "Strategies of Consultation." In W. G. Bennis, K. D. Benne, R. Chin, and K. E. Corey (Eds.), *The Planning of Change.* New York: Holt, Rinehart and Winston, 1976.

56

Conyne, R. K., and others. "The Environment as Client: Considerations and Implications for Counseling Psychology." Paper presented at American Psychological Association meeting, San Francisco, 1977.

Harvey, T. R. "Some Future Directions for Student Personnel Administration." *Journal of College Student Personnel,* 1974, *15* (4), 243–247.

Kurpius, D. "Consultation Theory and Process: An Integrated Model." *Personnel and Guidance Journal,* 1978, *56* (3), 335–338.

Lippitt, R., and Lippitt, G. "Consulting Process in Action." In J. E. Jones and J. W. Pfiffer (Eds.), *The 1977 Annual Handbook for Group Facilitators.* LaJolla, University Associates, 1977.

Martorana, S. V., and Kuhns, E. *Managing Academic Change: Interactive Forces and Leadership in Higher Education.* San Francisco: Jossey-Bass, 1975.

McGehearty, L. "The Case for Consultation." *Personnel and Guidance Journal,* 1968, *48,* 355–361.

Miller, T. K., and Prince, J. S. *The Future of Student Affairs: A Guide to Student Development for Tomorrow's Higher Education.* San Francisco: Jossey-Bass, Inc., 1976.

Morrill, W. E., and Banning, J. H. *Counseling Outreach: A Survey of Practices.* Boulder, Col.: Western Interstate Commission on Higher Education, 1973.

O'Bannion, T., and Thurstone, A. *Student Development Program in the Community College.* Englewood Cliffs, New Jersey: Prentice-Hall, 1972.

Parker, C. A., and Morrill, W. "Student Development Alternatives." *Journal of College Student Personnel.* 1974, *15* (3), 163–167.

Pfeiffer, J. W., and Jones, J. G. "Ethical Considerations in Consulting." In J. E. Jones and J. W. Pfeiffer (Eds.), *The 1977 Annual Handbook for Group Facilitators.* La Jolla: University Associates, 1977.

Pyron, T. "The Consultant Role as an Organizational Activity of Student Personnel Workers." *Journal of College Student Personnel,* 1974, *15* (4), 265–270.

Shepard, H. A. "Rules of Thumb for Change Agents." Private communication, 1972.

Shore, M., and Golann, S. "Problems of Ethics in Community Mental Health: A Survey of Community Psychologists." *Community Mental Health Journal,* 1969, *5* (6), 452–460.

Tollefson, A. L. *New Approaches to College Student Development.* New York: Herman Sciences Press, 1975.

*James H. Banning is vice president for student affairs
and associate professor of counseling psychology at
Colorado State University. Earlier he served as vice chancellor
for student affairs at the University of Missouri-Columbia.
Although trained as a clinical psychologist, his current
interests are in organizational and environmental change.*

Counseling centers, and other student services agencies,
can best serve their constituents by acknowledging and
emphasizing the vast potential of preventive interventions.

mediated services:
making the whole more
than the sum of its parts

m. kathryn hamilton
charles j. meade

Counseling centers, like other student services agencies, have typically engaged in a wide variety of activities with the overarching goal of promoting student development. Like other agencies, counseling centers have often lacked a conceptual model clearly delineating goals and products, outlining steps to reach those goals, and ways to create those products. Direct service activities have been most clearly understood, most easily counted, and most often evaluated, while indirect services have been subsumed under many labels (consultation, outreach) with resulting blurry thinking and hazy goals. A key to pulling together agency goals and functions may lie in thinking of the agency as a human development expert for the university system, and of all agency activities as manifestations of that central role. Clarifying the place of indirect (mediated) services within that overall role is necessary if an agency is to have a congruent way of describing and fulfilling its objectives. This chapter will propose a way to bring together mediated services within an integrated conceptual structure and will suggest a six stage process for implementation of that structure. A university counseling center is used as an example, but we most definitely believe that the process is equally applicable to any student services agency.

New Directions for Student Services, 5, 1979

background

University counseling centers are subsystems of the university. Each center also functions as a subsystem of a larger professional system of counseling psychology, which is within the even more complex system of the mental health field. Changes in professional goals and identities have occurred recently within all three systems. These changes in many ways parallel each other, though the interaction is not always obvious. That interaction will be illustrated here, and underlying themes will be shown to be applicable to student services functioning.

Throughout the quarter century of the official existence of counseling psychology as a specialty, counseling psychologists have worked in counseling centers, and surveys have been done about the functioning of those centers. Recent articles suggest three major trends in the evolution of perceptions about counseling center functioning. First, vocational counseling has decreased in being perceived as an appropriate problem area to discuss with counselors (Kohlan, 1975); at least one study, moreover, found counselors relatively uninterested in providing vocational counseling (Graff and McLean, 1970). A second trend has been the attainment of a central status by personal counseling (Gelso, Karl, and O'Connell, 1972). Third, recent surveys show a slowly growing focus on activities usually grouped under the label "outreach" (Warnath, 1973; Morrill and Oetting, 1970). Most centers provide a mixture of these services, with the emphasis still on remedial services (Lombardi, 1974). However, the increased emphasis on preventive services and on outreach shows a growing willingness to acknowledge and to confront campus mental health issues in ways other than by traditional remedial interventions.

These changes in counseling center role parallel developments in the professional identity of counseling psychologists. The gradual change from seeing ourselves as primarily vocational/educational counselors toward a primary identification as personal counselors and, recently, as outreach experts and environmental consultants has been documented elsewhere (Wrenn, 1977; Huebner, 1977). This broadening of our professional role has been reflected in the values of those directing graduate programs (Hamilton, 1977). Clearly, these role changes interact with the evolution in counseling center role and functioning.

The history of the development of the field of psychopathology from a demonological perspective through adoption of a medical model to the present emphasis on sociocultural causes for "mental illness" has been described by Coleman (1976). Recent writing emphasizes the potential of two alternatives to the medical model approach to understanding deviant behavior: an educational model, which proposes that appropriate educational intervention can reshape deviant behavior which is learned; and a social model, which postulates that deviant behavior is primarily developed from the social context, thus requiring intervention in the environment (Bloom, 1977). In 1967, a Task Force on Community Mental Health was appointed by Division 27

(Community Psychology) of the American Psychological Association. Its charge was to review available theories and empirical information relevant to community mental health, to develop positions, and to suggest priorities for psychologists working in the mental health field. One striking conclusion reached by the Task Force was that secondary prevention (early detection and treatment of problems, thus preventing increased severity) had generally been unsuccessful. The Task Force most strongly recommended a shift to placing the highest priority on primary prevention (preventing disorders from developing at all) and further suggested that this could best be accomplished by focusing on the facilitation of developmental tasks (Glidewell, 1971). This landmark event in the mental health field validates and parallels the increasing move in student services toward a broad student development perspective which emphasizes providing the best possible environment in which students can master developmental tasks.

Though the mental health field in general and counseling centers in particular continue to have a strong emphasis on remedial interventions (tertiary and secondary prevention), there is a steady growth of efforts in the primary prevention area and an increase in working with groups and systems rather than only with the individual showing "deviance". Group therapy and family therapy are increasingly prominent treatment modalities. Community psychology, though struggling with a lack of total acceptance, is gaining power (Iscoe, Bloom, and Spielberger, 1977). In personality theory there is a new emphasis on the interactional approach—the study of personality through the continuous complex interaction between an individual and his/her environment. Thus research and treatment must have a constant focus on the person, the situation, and the interaction between the two systems (Endler and Magnusson, 1976). Research on assessment of and intervention in environments is flourishing (Bloom, 1977). This is also consistent with the growing ecological perspective in student services (Tollefson, 1975).

It seems important to discuss counseling center functioning within the context of the counseling psychology field and within the larger context of the mental health field since all three systems interact. Clearly, counseling centers and counseling psychologists reflect the changes in the broad arena of mental health. It would be a mistake to examine the current status and future directions of campus mental health agencies in isolation. The above brief review validates the appropriateness of a general systems theory approach to conceptualizing campus mental health and human development services. The metamorphosis of each of the three systems seems to reflect a key concept of general systems theory, a unifying insight: that "the human being is an organized system, suspended in multiple systems, large and small, of physical, social, economic, and cultural type, and that his mental health depends on the effectiveness of the system operations that govern his relationship with the larger systems in which he exists" (Gray, 1972, p. 126).

This review of the history of the move toward a community/systems orientation for mental health services—both on and off campus—is focused on counseling centers. However, the basic trends and new assumptions clearly relate to the goals of all student services agencies and organizations which accept a student development orientation. The relative ease of tracing the trends in the mental health literature reflects the unfortunate fact that student services professionals have not adequately traced their history, have not clearly pulled together a direction in as integrated a way as have community psychologists. Such integration is necessary if we are to achieve excellence in building campus communities which foster optimal development of their inhabitants.

Systems Approach. Thinking of a counseling center or any other student services agency as a system serving another system — the campus community — suggests a necessary, continuous focus on the overall state of the community and of the service agency. It suggests an emphasis on multilevel system interventions whenever possible; it stresses awareness of potential effects of individual interventions on other subsystems besides the one(s) directly affected. For example, an intervention with an academic faculty which improved its cohesiveness might have positive effects on other departments within the same college by providing a model of colleague cohesiveness. That cohesiveness, however, could bring about increased interfaculty socialization and collaboration, reducing contact with and support of graduate students in the department. It is imperative that student services staff be aware that every intervention has multiple effects, and be willing to look for unexpected as well as predicted effects when evaluating interventions.

We would here propose that the systems approach to campus mental health and human development offers the most potential for positive impact on the campus community, and that a consistent "multilevel awareness" or "seeing the big picture" attitude will enhance the success of secondary and tertiary prevention and make primary prevention a reality. Willingness to intervene in the environment or at the institutional/organizational level means willingness to interact — to consult — with individuals and groups throughout the campus as needed. This is true for counseling centers and for all student services agencies. The theory and techniques usually included under the label of consultation are, then, keys to maximizing our effectiveness (Huebner, 1977). What is the current status of involvement and competence in consultation on campus?

Consultation in Counseling Centers. Eight years ago, several models of university counseling centers were described (Oetting, Ivey, and Weigel, 1970): the traditional (or jack-of-all-trades) model, the vocational guidance model, the psychotherapy model, the personnel services model, the academic affairs model, the training model, the research model, and the consultation model. The consultation model is based on the concept that "professionally trained people are too difficult to obtain and too valuable to use entirely for providing service" (p. 35; the authors were referring to direct service). The authors discussed advantages and disadvantages of this relatively *avant garde* model, including its applicability to primary prevention and evaluation. There has been a recent surge of interest in consultation activities of centers, though few of them seem to adhere closely to the consultation model discussed by these authors.

A more recent study (Gelso and others, 1977) has documented a discrepancy between student services workers and other relevant campus groups in their relative valuing of four of Oetting's, Ivey's, and Weigel's (1970) models for counseling centers. In a study on a large eastern campus, these researchers found that counseling center staff, resident assistants, and student personnel administrators thought consultation/outreach activities quite appropriate for the counseling center; students, faculty, and university administrators did not view consultation as an important function. We would suggest that a similar gap might exist on many campuses, among different subgroups within student services, and even within some center staffs.

A second factor which has kept the picture of campus consultation ambiguous is the fact that staffs conceptualize and practice consultation in a variety of ways. A recent survey (Hamilton, 1978) investigated attitudes and practices of 209 university and college counseling centers with regard to consultation. Respondents were directors of centers or staff members identified as primarily responsible for that functional area. Virtually all (96 percent) stated that they engaged in campus consultation, and 48 percent noted that they engaged in consultation to their local communities as well. The average length of time that these agencies had been providing consultation services was eight years. Centers reported devoting an average of 14 percent of staff time to consultation, and seven percent of the budget; 57 percent publicized consultation services. Clearly, counseling centers are active as consultants to their campus communities. Ambiguity arises when respondents report virtually every indirect service they provide under the general label of consultation. Activities including outreach, out-of-agency training, lectures and presentations, program development, organizational development, systems interventions, case consultation, and internal consultation to their own agencies were all seen by at least some respondents (range: 50 percent for systems interventions to 73 percent for case consultation and program development) as "consultation." Obviously, there is a lack of clarity regarding what consultation entails.

Yet another factor inhibiting the potential of counseling centers to serve as campus consultants is the issue, ever present for counseling centers and all service agencies, of the tension between direct remedial service (serving the walking wounded) and preventive/developmental interventions which are hard to evaluate and difficult to justify. Every service agency is familiar with this conflict, though it may not be discussed openly. Consultation or preventive goals are often defined but abandoned when direct service or remedial demands increase. This is a difficult issue for staffs to deal with openly; however, it is important not to make decisions about goals and resource allocation by default.

Finally, though most centers report much activity in the consultation area, they usually lack a theoretical framework and a clear administrative structure within which to plan and carry out goals. The 1977 survey (Hamilton, 1978) found only 21 percent of respondents reporting any model whatsoever for categorizing their activities in this area, and only 34 percent reported regularly defining objectives. Further, only 28 percent reported having an individual or team primarily responsible for consultation. Regular evaluation of activities reported ranged from a dismal nine percent (for case consultation) to a high of 43 percent (for outreach). Clearly, there is a tendency to fragment functioning in the consultation sphere and a need for integration of goals and activities.

clarification of terms: a proposal

We would propose that the label of "consultation" be applied only to activities which clearly fit within the traditional definition of consultation as a voluntary helping relationship in which the consultant provides some kind of expertise to the consultee (Lippitt, 1959). For counseling centers and other student services agencies which provide a broad range of services to their campuses we would propose that those services be conceptualized within two major areas. The first, direct service, would include traditional remedial interventions and other services provided directly to students, such as certain developmental programs. Services which *in any way* are provided indirectly, or mediated through an individual (for example, case consultation with a resident assistant about how to handle a problem student on the floor) or an organization (for example, administrative consultation with an academic department to improve retention of ethnic minorities) would be categorized under the label *mediated services* (Margolis, Sorenson and Galane, 1977). This way of thinking and operating has a number of important advantages.

First, the label ties together diverse activities by emphasizing their common denominator—providing *service* to the campus, service which is mediated through a person or group. This semantic change is useful in that it reminds staff and community that indirect interventions are services, and as such deserve equivalent consideration to direct services. Second, it allows a reduction in the number of times the term consultation is used; this can be a loaded word. Many indirect services are consultations—and many are collaborative efforts. Doubtless, a great amount of tension between various student services agencies can be eliminated if staff can clarify the difference between the two; in too many cases, one agency may see itself as consulting to another, while the "consultee" views itself as an equal collaborator. According to our definition of mediated services, many such services are neither consultation nor collaboration. Third, by combining indirect services, it is possible to more clearly build a conceptual framework for planning them. Acknowledgment of mediated services as one of two major products of an agency (direct and indirect services) makes it possible to conceptualize, plan, and evaluate activities as part of an overall area of function. This, again, allows staff to have a continuous focus on the whole picture of the campus and on the agency's impact on campus, facilitating a productive, integrated systems approach.

The above background and report of the current status of consultation/mediated services on campus suggests three major needs if student services agencies are to integrate and enhance their mediated activities. The most pressing need seems to be for agencies to discuss the difficult issues and values questions, to decide the level of commitment they wish to make to mediated services, to set goals and evaluate progress toward them—to be aware and planful. Second, more consistent monitoring and feedback about indirect activities is crucial for accountability and evaluation needs. Finally, it may be necessary, if an agency wishes to make a commitment to setting a high priority on mediated interventions, to educate the consumers of those interventions (Gelso and others, 1977).

model: the counseling center as
human development expert for the campus

We believe that campus counseling centers as well as other student services agencies have an opportunity to take leadership in providing a truly integrated set of human services. Counseling psychologists have produced excellent models for multilevel, multimethod, multitarget interventions; the most comprehensive, and the most appropriate for counseling centers, seems to be the cube model of Morrill, Oetting, and Hurst (1974). The problem is that although the model has existed, with variations, for some years now, we are not filling all the squares on the cube. We are not working in an integrated way, though we are doing many bits and pieces, to provide the broad spectrum of services that we have so strongly espoused. The concept of mediated services, combined with the traditional idea of direct service, offers a means of putting together all the pieces into a meaningful, coherent whole.

As counseling psychologists, we have the tradition of a developmental and preventive and remedial stance; we have excellent models; we have most, though perhaps not all, of the skills to provide the full range of interventions we discuss in our professional literature. We have identified ourselves as specialists who can work with virtually the full range of psychological functioning, from disturbed individuals to normal populations; we have expressed willingness and interest to work with organizations and environments as well as with individuals and groups. We have, some might say, even been smug about our qualifications to do these things. It is more important to be effective than to be smug; it is more important to try some of the models, to implement some of the ideals, than to further refine our theoretical models while we continue to provide primarily remedial services and make mediated services a sort of stepchild.

On many campuses the counseling center is the primary mental health agency. Whether or not it is defined administratively as the coordinator of all psychological services, its staff have a responsibility to clearly define their desired role on campus and to move toward that. Consultation skills, in role definition and goal attainment, are crucial. The existence of other student services offices which may provide some similar services, or the existence (or nonexistence) of other psychological facilities, will affect decisions made by center staff about the degree of investment in various areas. However, we propose that the center staff are obligated in most cases, because of existing expertise across a wide range of services, to assume a central responsibility for providing an integrated, full service package.

Let us define the kind of human development expert model we are proposing for counseling centers. It is similar to, yet broader than, the consultative model described by Oetting, Ivey, and Weigel (1970). Some basic assumptions are necessary for such a model. First, the campus would be seen as an open system, with variably permeable boundaries and a constantly changing population. Second, the counseling center would see itself as a human development expert for the campus community as a whole. The center using this model would continue to provide traditional direct services — therapy and counseling, developmental programs, career services, testing. However, there would be a primary commitment to the use of consultation, to mediated interventions, and to prevention. Mediated services would be as highly valued as direct services and would be planned on a longrange basis. Inservice and graduate student training would see acquisition of relevant theory and skills equally important as skills in the direct service area. Research and evaluation would be integral parts of assessing mediated interventions. Of critical importance would be a commitment to the use of continuous, sophisticated, and appropriately varied needs assessments as a way of tailoring mediated interventions to changing needs.

Thus, the counseling center (like other student services agencies) is a consultant to, or expert for, the campus community regarding the emotional health and development of students and perhaps others. Here is a role and value issue: many centers see themselves as responsible for serving students only, while others visualize their responsibility as an obligation to serve the entire community and all its inhabitants, including faculty and staff. Still others are mandated or choose to serve their communities beyond the campus. When there is significant disagreement *within* a center about who comprises the primary target population, there is much room for explicit and implicit conflict.

Many agencies currently provide many or most of the pieces of the above picture right now; what seems to be lacking for many is a conscious, overall plan. Where do mediated interventions fit in? How do they contribute to the overall functioning of the agency? How might an agency move toward increased coherence of efforts? We would suggest an outline for a process by which an agency might develop a plan to achieve the model we have described. The process would be useful for any center or student services agency which wanted to more clearly articulate its direction and allocate its resources, even without the goal of reaching the high level of involvement in mediated services which we propose.

A key concept in planning agency goals, again, is in seeing the agency as a constantly changing system. In moving through the process outlined here, staff must continually assess the current functioning of their system and of the effects of the process on that system. The process starts with looking at the overall state of the agency and goals for service, and then focuses on mediated services goals and ways of implementation.

The potential ambiguity of goals and activities in this area and the frequent ambivalence about commitment to mediated services as a core function make it advisable to create a means of introducing mediated services as a legitimate, clearly defined functional area within the agency. This plan was created for and piloted by a university counseling center. Most or all aspects, however, are applicable to any student services agency active in mediated interventions. Each stage will be discussed separately.

Stage 1: Defining basic assumptions and goals; constructing the machinery. In many ways this is the most important stage. It has two parts, the first of which involves clarifying assumptions. Here the staff generates a list of underlying assumptions about their work; the task is to find a list on which everyone can agree as a clearly defined common denominator. It is helpful to use stimulus questions to start discussion: Given the impossibility of seeing every potential client, what is the best way to serve students and the campus? What is the obligation to the campus community as a whole? How important is the commitment to prevention? The staff at the university in question agreed on the following basic assumptions:

- We have a commitment to the entire student population.
- Intervention should be preventive as well as remedial.
- We should actively seek those who may need assistance but have not asked for it; aim for all students to know about our services.
- We should provide educational opportunities relative to developmental needs.
- We should respond to complex mental health issues with an appropriately complex and diverse intervention plan.
- We have responsibilities to serve administration, faculty, and staff as consultants and by offering supportive services.
- We have responsibility to train others and ourselves.
- We have responsibility to know what is expected of us by the campus community and to respond accordingly.
- We have responsibility to take leadership in identifying and coordinating mental health resources on campus.

The staff was unable to unanimously agree on the statement "we have a responsibility to the entire campus community," so it was not adopted. However, the mediated services coordinator continues to offer that as a valid assumption periodically!

In this process of defining assumptions, long-standing issues may emerge and require difficult discussion. Conflicting values may exist; this is not necessarily a problem. All staff should be able to define at least some areas of agreement, possibly with a goal to enlarge them. Agreement about general goals and values allows those implementing them later to have sanction; it reduces the potential for sabotage. The process may be illuminating and have added benefits of increasing cohesiveness, or of generating enthusiasm in staff who are burning out.

Next, staff can talk about goals to serve the assumptions. Examples of general goals might be: "creating an ideal balance between external requests for service and internally initiated services," "setting time and money goals for mediated services," and so on. Goals defined here should be global. The most important outcome of this part of Stage 1 is clarity of values and a sense of commitment to mediated interventions.

The second part of this stage concerns administrative structures to serve the goals. Two needs exist. The first is to identify the place of mediated services in the organizational structure of the agency. Often, "consultation" has not had a place on the organizational chart, or has shifted around from year to year, or has lacked a person or team to provide coordination. Here, mediated service was defined, with direct service, as one of two *products* of the agency and both were included together on the organizational chart. The second need is the naming of an individual or group responsible for administering the functional area. The individual or team can then take responsibility for moving the agency through the other five stages of the process.

Stage 2: Mapping the Agency. Environmental mapping, cognitive mapping — these are terms used frequently these days by student services professionals. As a system serving the university system, the counseling center must have an accurate picture of its internal resources. Staff should be able to clearly stage their individual and collective expertise in areas related to mediated services. For senior staff, this may entail a structured reassessment of their current skill level, past training and experiences. Some may be ambivalent about this, feeling that their competence is in question. We suggest that this process is essential because of the acknowledged lack of formal preparation of counseling psychologists in several critical areas: consultation, environmental assessment, outreach, program evaluation. Staff can help each other minimize defensive reactions. Assessment of other resources — time, money, facilities, interests — is also necessary. Then staff members can determine their individual commitments to mediated interventions for a particular period, probably a year.

Stage 3: Mapping the Environment. Having a clear idea of internal resources, goals, and commitments, the staff must next assess available resources within the campus environment. There are three kinds of mapping. First, the staff forms a picture of individual and agency relationships with each subsystem in the campus community. This was done here by the mediated services coordinator; individual interviews with senior staff, going through the university organizational chart section by section, generated information about current and past professional and personal relationships with members of all academic and administrative units. This is a fascinating and instructive way to see what kind of pattern a center has (perhaps inadvertently) established over the years in making liaisons. The information can be summarized graphically, on the chart, and the data quantified to produce rankings of the intensity and quality of relationships with persons and organizations. This allowed the center for the first time to have a comprehensive overview of its level of involvement with the system as a whole. Productive use of such "networks" is a key component of successful consultation (Sarason, 1976). The anecdotal information also proves useful over time.

The second kind of mapping entails reviewing other resources on campus which could be helpful to the agency in providing service. Other student services professionals, for example, have skills in programming or consultation which offer potential for collaboration, thus minimizing duplication of service and reducing amount of staff time from each agency. Again, the staff had a general idea of the nature of those skills, but reviewing the whole picture—like reviewing staff skills and campus relationships—allowed a more coherent, complete picture of the array of resources.

Finally, a third area to map is the area of administrative support for mediated services. A key administrator can have great impact on a center's ability to provide them. Many professionals committed to preventive/ mediated interventions may cite an administrator, director, or colleague as unmoveable barrier to their goals, but we suggest that that may be simplistic and motivated by an external locus of control. The responsibility for getting adequate financial, administrative, and professional support lies nowhere but with ourselves. It would be ironic if we projected a vision of social change brought about by our skills while claiming that the person, group, or institution which we have the most opportunity to change is unchangeable. If there is an inadequate level of support, a priority may be set to educate that administrator, or governing body, about the importance of a full range of services and of prevention.

Stage 4: Review and Planning. In this stage, the core staff reviews the total picture in light of projected needs, environmental and staff data, and overall direct and mediated goals. General priorities are set, based on the previous assumptions and goals. The agency should be able to formulate a specific plan for the mediated services area. Beginning a conscious move toward more investment in mediated services necessitates thinking several years ahead; a short-term, perhaps one year, plan for the first level of objectives would probably be appropriate.

For example, a staff might make a commitment to increased use of media to publicize services and to do educational/preventive interventions. Creating training films for resident assistants could be a task for the first year. This project would serve a variety of goals. It would provide improved service to students in contact with the resident assistants, thus serving an immediate need. Staff would be able to use the films as a pilot project to gain competence with the use of film, and would have ample opportunity to evaluate the impact. The next year staff might build on this by implementing a second film project with faculty advisors, thus responding to a present need within the context of a longitudinal plan for increasing media interventions.

In addition to planning specific interventions, staff might now choose which liaison relationships needed most focus during the coming year, either to improve an existing relationship or to initiate a contact where there is none. For example, a staff might perceive a deficit in the relationship with the campus police which possibly impedes service to students by minimizing communication; a staff member could volunteer to begin a regular contact with a key member of the police staff. The point is that agencies can easily fall into a pattern of being reactive in their relationships with the campus community, or can focus only on student services colleagues. We propose that it is a responsibility of the agency to assess potential intervention points and to build relationships which lay groundwork for effective service later.

Another task of this stage is to assess staff training needs and to plan training for the year.

Thus, the major objective of this stage is to set clear goals for the time period in question, always keeping in mind longterm goals. Evaluation and accountability planning are also most appropriately done at this stage. In addition to deciding which activities fit within the mediated services area, many agencies may find it useful to choose a theoretical model to categorize mediated interventions for ease in conceptualizing and in counting. The center here uses an expanded Caplanian model (Caplan, 1970). Morrill, Oetting, and Hurst's (1974) cube also would be appropriate for most student services agencies.

Stage 5: Implementation. In this stage, mediated services team members and other staff develop and carry out planned interventions. Using the general guidelines and goals chosen by the staff, the team makes dispositions of requests in the area and initiates programs. Throughout the allocated time period, the mediated services coordinator works closely with the direct services coordinator to monitor agency resource allocation; with the evaluation coordinator; and with the director, to have his/her perspective on the effects of campus administrative or political issues on mediated services. The team keeps the staff informed of important developments in the area and, if necessary, goals or priorities are renegotiated.

Stage 6: Evaluative Review. At the end of the designated time period, the core staff reviews mediated services activities as part of an overall review. Successes and failures are discussed; new priorities are defined, always with the aim to continue integrating this area with other functional areas within the agency.

A staff can use this process continuously; after the initial time, Stages 1, 2, and 3 may be less time-consuming. However, regular review of overall goals and assumptions, and updating of staff and campus resources, are necessary to maintain focused and realistic direction for the provision of mediated services.

summary

College and university campuses present special obstacles to positive system change; these obstacles (for example, the self-perpetuating nature of the educational system, the pressure on faculty members to engage in conventional and isolated work in order to receive promotion, unwieldy and constricting financial structures) make institutional intervention complex and sometimes frustrating (Adelson, 1974). Counseling center staff or other student services professionals attempting to intervene are faced with special complications because they are internal consultants and may have multiple relationships with those whom they wish to influence (Lanning, 1974; Warnath, 1971; Westbrook and others, 1978). However, there are many positive aspects to having consultants involved with consultee systems over a period of years (McGreevy, 1978) and in that aspect the counseling center and its staff occupy a position with unique advantages for their ability to have ongoing effects on their campus communities. The goals of counseling centers and of all student services—the fuller development of the university community and its inhabitants — are congruent with the idea of building a competent community as expressed by community psychologists (Iscoe, 1974).

This chapter emphasizes viewing the counseling center and other student services agencies as human systems which, like any other human systems, are organismic in nature and as such are able to develop and evolve over time (Bertalanffy, 1968). Any proposal such as the one provided here must be seen as a point in time statement; we must maintain the flexibility to evaluate and respond to needs on a continuous basis. At some time in the future, it may be that a human development expert model would be inappropriate. At this time, our proposal appears to hold the most potential for providing appropriate, flexible, integrated, and effective service to the university systems we want to affect.

references

Adelson, M. "On Changing Higher Education from Within." *American Behavioral Scientist*, 1974, *18*, 232–249.

Bertalanffy, L. *General System Theory*. New York: George Braziller, 1968.

Bloom, B. L. *Community Mental Health—A General Introduction*. Monterey: Brooks/Cole, 1977.

Caplan, G. *The Theory and Practice of Mental Health Consultation*. New York: Basic Books, 1970.

Coleman, J. C. *Abnormal Psychology and Modern Life*. Glenview, Ill.: Scott, Foresman and Co., 1976.

Endler, N. S., and Magnusson, D. *Interactional Psychology and Personality*. New York: Wiley, 1976.

Gelso, C. J., Karl, N. J., and O'Connell, T. "Perceptions of the Role of a University Counseling Center." *Journal of College Student Personnel*, 1972, *13*, 441–447.

Gelso, C. J., and others. "A Multigroup Evaluation of the Models and Functions of University Counseling Centers." *Journal of Counseling Psychology*, 1977, *24* (4), 338–348.

Glidewell, J. "Priorities for Psychologists in Community Mental Health." In Division 27, American Psychological Assn., Task Force on Community Mental Health, *Issues in Community Psychology and Preventive Mental Health*. New York: Behavioral Publications, 1971.

Graff, R., and McLean, D. "Evaluating Educational-Vocational Counseling: A Model for Change." *Personnel and Guidance Journal*, 1970, *48*, 568–574.

Gray, W. "Bertalanffian Principles as a Basis for Humanistic Psychiatry." In Laszlo, E. (Ed.), *The Relevance of General Systems Theory*. New York: George Braziller, 1972.

Hamilton, M. K. "Graduate Training and Professional Identity." *The Counseling Psychologist*, 1977, *7* (2), 26–29.

Hamilton, M. K. "Survey of Consultation Activities in College Counseling Centers." Fort Collins: University Counseling Center, Colorado State University, 1978.

Huebner, L. A. "Counseling Interventions: An Organizational-Interactional Approach." *The Counseling Psychologist*, 1977, *7* (2), 69–73.

Iscoe, I. "Community Psychology and the Competent Community." *American Psychologist*, 1974, *29* (7), 607–613.

Iscoe, I., Bloom, B. L., and Spielberger, C. D. *Community Psychology in Transition*. Washington, D.C.: Hemisphere Publishing Corporation, 1977.

Kohlan, R. G. "Problems Appropriate for Discussion in Counseling Centers: 15 Years Later." *Journal of Counseling Psychology,* 1975, *22,* 560-562.

Lanning, W. "An Expanded View of Consultation for College and University Counseling Centers." *Journal of College Student Personnel,* 1974, *15* (3), 171-176.

Lippitt, R. "Dimensions of the Consultant's Job." *Journal of Social Issues,* 1959, *15* (2), 5-12.

Lombardi, J. S. "The College Counseling Center and Preventive Mental Health Activities." *Journal of College Student Personnel,* 1974, *15* (6), 435-438.

McGreevy, C. P. "Training Consultants: Issues and Approaches." *Personnel and Guidance Journal,* 1978, *56* (7), 432-435.

Margolis, R. B., Sorensen, J. L., and Galane, J. "Consumer Satisfaction in Mental Health Delivery Services." *Professional Psychology,* 1977, *8* (1), 11-16.

Morrill, W. H., and Oetting, E. R. "Outreach Programs in College Counseling." *Journal of College Student Personnel,* 1970, *11* (1), 50-53.

Morrill, W. H., Oetting, E. R., and Hurst, J. C. "Dimensions of Counselor Functioning." *Personnel and Guidance Journal,* 1974, *52,* 354-359.

Oetting, E. R., Ivey, A. E., and Weigel, R. G. *The College and University Counseling Center.* Student Personnel Series No. 11. Washington, D.C.: American College Personnel Association, 1970.

Sarason, S. "Community Psychology, Networks, and Mr. Everyman." *American Psychologist,* 1976, *31,* 317-328.

Tollefson, A. L. *New Approaches to College Student Development.* New York: Human Sciences Press, 1975.

Warnath, C. F. *New Myths and Old Realities: College Counseling in Transition.* San Francisco: Jossey-Bass, 1971.

Warnath, C. F. *New Directions for College Counselors: A Handbook for Redesigning Professional Roles.* San Francisco: Jossey-Bass, 1973.

Westbrook, F. D., and others. "University Campus Consultation Through the Formation of Collaborative Dyads." *Personnel and Guidance Journal,* 1978, *56* (6), 359-363.

Wrenn, C. G. "Landmarks and the Growing Edge." *The Counseling Psychologist,* 1977, *7* (2), 10-13.

M. Kathryn Hamilton is senior psychologist at the University Counseling Center and assistant professor of psychology at Colorado State University.

Charles J. Meade is assistant professor of counseling psychology and coordinator of consultation in the University Counseling Service at the University of Iowa.

Two student services administrators present differing views
on the role of consultation in the university community.

summary: two views

w. harry sharp
james c. hurst

The complexities of consultation may sometimes be seen most clearly by student services administrators whose task is to see "the whole picture." In this chapter, two such persons present contrasting views of the role of consultation within student services. The preceding chapters have presented the practitioners' perspective on the benefits and pitfalls of consultation. These authors, speaking from one of the most inclusive levels of the university system, raise a number of issues concerning the pros and cons of intersystem consultation within the university. Sharp's view is that the formalizing and public labeling of consultation efforts by student services personnel may have a number of deleterious consequences. Hurst, on the other hand, views the systematization of consultation efforts by student services as the keystone which will integrate the various identities of student services personnel into a meaningful gestalt. These two views capture current dynamic tension within the area of consultation, between those who see it as fraught with danger and political turmoil and those who view it as a potent source of change.

let the consultant beware

w. harry sharp

The consultative role played by student services personnel is needed and desirable. The role is not a new one for the student services worker. It is merely a matter of client and role redefinition. Having raised my hand on the "yea" side, let me state that the "yea" is qualified.

the issue

Be Formal and Beware. To systematize *formally* and to label *publicly* the consultative role of a university student services agency may not be economically or politically prudent. Most assuredly, the agency must have its consultative roles systematized. If not, the staff would not understand their professional roles or the programmatic objectives of the agency. However, to formalize and label publicly the consultative role has far-reaching implications for all concerned. There are many assumptions that need be acknowledged and addressed before an agency can viably move into this role dimension. The staff must agree that this is an appropriate activity for them and must have the necessary expertise needed to carry out such a new program.

At the administrative level, formalization and labeling assumes that job functions and personnel records have been changed in order to reflect appropriate levels of responsibility. Formalization and labeling assumes that the decisions about appropriate personnel classifications and any accompanying salary adjustments have been determined. Responsibility and accountability for the consultative function will have been established clearly. Formalization and labeling assumes that the consultative role has been acknowledged by the appropriate university administrators. For example, the counseling center may *assume* that all the responsible parties have agreed that it should serve in an official consultative function on the campus; in fact, the center may be prone to assume or act as if the campus as a totality had decided. We may be assured that such a decision within central administration would have specified the scope of the consultative role and limits would have been established.

If, in this example, counseling center programs (like academic programs) had to survive the plethora of departmental and divisional committee reviews plus the scrutiny of campus wide committees and councils, one wonders how the formalization of the consultative role would be received. Unfortunately, new administrative programs, including student services programs, may have only been evaluated or appraised by other administrative units which may pit agency priorities against overall university priorities. Unfortunately, all too often, the campus wide political support is not gained through such an administrative process and we err by assuming it.

Keep Out, It's Mine. Formalizing and labeling also has important implications for issues of territoriality and ownership within a division of student services. For example certain faculty and staff will consider the counseling center to be the agency of mental health expertise on campus, others may gravitate to the psychiatry department or hospital, and still others may turn to other mental health personnel (campus ministers, student health services). Others will seek out friends or colleagues. Such diversity of expertise breeds potential divisiveness, particularly if an agency begins to see itself as possessing the "real" experts and advertises as such, creating a new identity of (in this example) Mental Health Consultant.

Similar battles are imaginable in a number of areas. Will we now have Career Consultation, Test Construction Consultation, Admission and Retention Consultation, Teacher Effectiveness Consultation, Residence Hall Consultation, Intra- and Inter-Departmental Conflict Consultation, Student Development Consultation? Which student service offices will want to do which part? What should be the limits on the consultation role? How will the campus react to such a formalization and titling of areas of expertise?

Some will say that I nit-pick and exaggerate. I believe the consultation role of student services personnel needs to be accomplished in a slightly different mode. Obviously, I shun the formalization and labeling of consultation services. Once we publicly tag ourselves as a Consultant, others do expect an expert.

Being perceived as a helping colleague and friend, a peer, carries quite different implications than being perceived as an expert. I do not believe I am splitting semantic hairs. I admit that my approach to consultation is slightly seductive but, I believe, genuine. Departmental territories are less critical if I am perceived as a colleague and peer. Personal feelings and relationships are involved as opposed to professional and political entities. My peers, as my students, are free to seek assistance or not. They may reject or accept my advice. I do not bear the title Consultant. My expertise will be judged on its own merits. I am free to be something less than expert. I am a professional who is concerned about the welfare of students. I may facilitate change on campus in the usual procedural modes. I am an integral part of the campus. I am not set apart as is a Consultant.

the participants

The Consultee's Point of View. Universities are accustomed to making use of consultants. This almost always means an outsider or group of outsiders hired for a specific fee. As a user of such consultants, I can tell you that there have been some I wished had tarried for a while and some who were on campus for an eternity. But always, I could bid them farewell with, at least, appropriate monetary thanks. I could make use of their consultation in any way I chose. I did not feel any constraints on accepting or rejecting the consultative advice. Personal relationships did not interfere with my judgmental and decision making processes.

If the on-campus, official consultant is a colleague, a friend, and perhaps even a neighbor, the dynamics are quite different between my Consultant and me. As long as we have a third party to discuss, a troubled student, we probably are on fairly safe ground. But let us assume that the consultation has to do with my staff, with the functions or functioning of my office, with my grading or teaching techniques. Now my consultant and I may have difficulties depending on my needs and/or my level of resistance. Hell, maybe I did not even want to see the damned Consultant in the first place, but my dean or department head had made such a suggestion—a most pointed one. Student service agencies have always worried about the relationship with their clients. All theories of counseling, for example, speak to the counselor—client relationship and to the desirability of accepting clients on a voluntary basis only. Now I am not working with transient expert consultant but a permanent member of the community, the consultant, and the relationship is less than voluntary.

The Consultant's Point of View. If the consultative role has been formalized, the program is open to challenge. If the consultative role is based on collegiality and camaraderie then only the individual can be challenged. Colleagues and friends, as entities, are usually not challenged during the process of budgetary review. Programs often *are* challenged, particularly if cost effectiveness and/or accountability cannot be demonstrated. Programs are most assuredly challenged when others, particularly faculty, are after the same monies.

How many rejections, for whatever reason, can we as professionals and experts tolerate on our own campus? When we establish ourselves as the experts in relationship to our peers, what have we accomplished, dynamically, on our campus? This is particularly important for those most likely to advertise themselves as the Consultant. They often are those with the doctorate who hold academic rank, such as the staff of a counseling center. Such people may well be resented by their student service peers and their faculty peers and need to recognize and deal with this potential resistance.

the solution

Let's Not Formalize—Let's Just Do It. As with counseling, consultation, if successful, will initiate change. The consultee who has had the process imposed will resist change in the same manner as a client who has been forced to see a counselor. As a consultant dealing with an administrative unit, one should recognize that all professionals in the unit want change in varying degrees. Not only that, but the desired nature of the change may vary within the group. Some may even prize the *status quo!*

Outside consultants often recognize and recommend organizational and administrative structural changes, personnel changes, increased or decreased staffing patterns, physical improvements or additions. Hopefully explicit or implicit within each consultative task is a keen awareness of and concern for students. How will the on-campus consultant handle such judgments? What will be the reception on campus of such judgments? The consultant has been isolated from the traditional committee process. By definition, a consultant is not a part of a committee or council. The consultant stands administratively alone. If the consultant's recommendation angers a portion of the campus, will the consultant be permitted to consult again with significant persons? Depending on the power structure and the political climate of the campus, the answer is "perhaps." If the consultant also serves as a counselor, will the members of the angered group seek out or even be willing to share their problems with this counselor?

If the consultation service has been formalized and labeled, will the consultant be accepted on appropriate campus committees? How can one be both a committee member and a Consultant? The Consultant's new role may entail an advisory (staff rather than line) relationship. Certainly, the staff designation may have advantages as well as disadvantages.

An additional significant point needs to be made concerning the campus' perception and acceptance of the consultant. Universities and colleges, both faculty and administrative personnel, have an abundance of people who are engaged regularly in the business of consultation. One need not visit a campus to validate this fact. One needs only to spend time with a member of the state legislature, the governing board, or a graduate. The campuses of our nation are truly blessed with experts and available consultants! The appropriate committee structure might well make use of this expertise. Most assuredly a cost benefit would be realized.

Let me repeat that I sincerely believe in and, in fact, practice, informally and untitled, a consultative role on campus. The advantages through the formalization and titular process, I believe, are outweighed by the disadvantages.

An Example Or Two. A few cases may illustrate my point. A counseling and testing center has had a long established test scoring service for faculty. Faculty have asked for and received item analyses of examination results. They have requested and received assistance in the construction of examinations. Most recently faculty have inquired about assistance in the area of research design and methodology. The latter is a rather unusual consultative function for a university counseling center. This is particularly startling since such services have been formalized, labeled, and staffed with experts elsewhere on campus, who fall under the administrative purview of the chief academic administrator.

Maybe, just maybe, faculty do not like to admit their lack of information in this critical area. Publish or perish has had impact. The faculty who have quietly commented to the counseling center staff that they need help in the above area have expressed their related fear of the promotional and tenure decisions affecting them. Question: Would such fearful and admittedly ignorant faculty express these fears and self-perceived weaknesses in the office that has been formalized for the prescribed purpose? The reporting relationship of this latter office is significant.

A few years ago I was asked to visit a campus to propose and plan programs in a particular area of student services. At the end of the consultation visit with the responsible department head, I felt confident in advising the administrator who had hired me that the problem was the department head. I recommended the department head be terminated. If this same consultative request had happened on my campus, would I have acted as appropriately and as speedily? I am not sure that my personal feelings toward the professional involved would not have clouded the issue and my judgment. I do know that I would have required far more time to arrive at the recommendation for termination.

A Final Word. The consultant must remember that the campus is a highly charged political entity. The formalized and titled Consultant, performing the consultative function on his or her own campus, will find it difficult, if not impossible, to avoid campus political battles. Unlike governmental politics, which are quite overt, campus politics tend to be covert, but still ever present.

Again, let me state that the consultative role played by student services personnel is needed and desirable. Formalizing and publicly labeling such a function may have more serious consequences for the agency than performing the same functions informally with one's peers.

Let the consultant beware!

*W. Harry Sharp received his Ph.D. in
counseling psychology from Ohio State University.
In both his former role as the director of the University of
Wyoming Counseling Center and in his current capacity
as vice chancellor, dean of students at the University of Houston,
he has had extensive experience in doing consultation
and in coordinating consultative efforts among
a number of student service agencies.*

consultation and credibility
james c. hurst

As student services professionals, we are at our best when we are inter-
vening either directly in the lives of students, or indirectly in the educational
environment in which students are immersed. Intervention, of course, is not
an end in itself, but must be marked by explicit goals, intentional processes,
and thorough evaluations. Morrill, Oetting and Hurst (1974) developed a
three dimensional model useful in classifying and defining the characteristics
of therapeutic interventions. Their first dimension identified four classifications of targets or recipients of intended intervention. These are the *individual*, the *primary group*, the larger but more loosely knit *associational group*,
and the *institution or community* as a whole. The three purposes for which
intervention occurs are *remedial* (to repair damage already done), *preventative* (to counteract processes leading to damage), and *developmental* (to
maximize the potential of individuals and environments). The methods by
which interventions occur are classified as *direct* (where the professional is
immediately and personally involved in the intervention); *training* (of others
to intervene); *consultation* (with individuals, groups, or systems to prepare
them for self-sustaining action); and *media* (wherein films, videotapes, pro-
grammed modules and so on are developed for purposes of intervention).

It is essential that consultation be perceived as *one* method by which
intervention may occur. It is neither more nor less than that. Some over-
enthusiastic professionals (often with brand new skills in consultation) would
have us believe that consultation is the strategy by which student services will
finally acquire its long sought-after respectability in the world of academia.
This is not the case. Consultation is, however, one of the most potentially
effective methods for creating change in a complex system. It can be one of
the most powerful tools in the hands of a skilled professional, especially with
associational group and institutional targets.

prerequisites to competent consultation

One basic assumption that precedes all consulting contracts is that the
prospective consultant has some expertise in a skill or knowledge area and
competence in the process by which that expertise is transferred to the consultee. The traditional realm of expertise for the student services professionals
has been the specific knowledge related to the agency in which they work.
These agencies typically include financial aids, housing, counseling, unions,
health centers, recreational sports, offices of deans of students, admissions
and records, and others. With the advent of student development as the conceptual framework for student services has come the expectation that exper-

tise in the process of human development be added to the more traditional areas. A thorough knowledge of the developmental process during late adolescence and early adulthood will best prepare the student services professional for consultation with the general student population. Knowledge of the unique characteristics and needs of special student populations such as ethnic minorities, older returning students, students with disabilities, women, and veterans is necessary. Knowledge of intrapersonal development in the intellectual, emotional, cultural, moral, social and physical realms is also necessary. Without knowledge and expertise in the human development process the student services professional has no business offering to serve as a consultant on the subject. With that knowledge that same professional is prepared to assume his or her rightful place as a person on campus recognized as having current and accurate information concerning the attitudes, thinking, behavior and needs of general and specific student populations.

Although the importance of the environment in influencing human development is a well established fact, the student services profession has only recently become active in applying principles of environmental assessment and design to higher education. The basic task of systematically investigating matches and mismatches between student needs and environmental characteristics is not being claimed by any other component in higher education and is one of the potentially most productive arenas within which consultation may occur. Credibility can only be earned, however, through careful, defensible studies of students and their interaction with the environment. A high level of investigative skill and a strong knowledge base are particularly crucial because faculty and administration are integral parts of the student environment and could be identified as one element inhibiting the development of students. Consultation here is a high-risk, high-gain proposition with most thorough preparation necessary to reduce risk to an acceptable level.

The third prerequisite to effective consultation is competence in the process of consultation. Nothing interferes with the credibility of a consultant more than a hesitant entry, inaccurate diagnosis, faulty implementation, or awkward exit. Even the most expert knowledge and skill in student development and environmental assessment and design will be neutralized by an inadequate mastery of the consultation process. Various models of consultation have been presented in earlier chapters; consultants may find different models useful for various situations. However, the consultant must possess a thorough command of at least one model of consultation for purposes of planning and evaluating consultation and training others in consultation.

Although evaluation of consultation activity is a step included in most consultation models, it bears noting as a fourth prerequisite to consultation. The evaluation process really begins with or prior to the entry and is complete only when the data are incorporated into the beliefs and behaviors of the consultant. The feedback process is critical to the development of the individual as a consultant, the evaluation of the model itself, and the assessment of the impact of the intervention.

Finally, the importance of the self-confidence of the consultant is a key element. Student personnel curricula in the past have had a primarily applied emphasis, and training programs have reflected this lack of theoretical and scientific substance. Historically, the training programs also seem to have had a tendency to attract more than their share of graduate students not strong enough to compete in "content" areas. These factors have caused the field of student personnel to be crowded with a seemingly large number of professionals who lack the confidence to move assertively into academic colleges, departments and administrative units to intervene for human development. A solid foundation of knowledge and skill in human development, environmental assessment, student/environment interaction, the consultation process, and evaluation strategies along with a strong track record of personal success are necessary to create valid self-confidence for the consultant. Part of this can be provided through selection of candidates for graduate study in student personnel, the other through more rigorous education and training in the content and skills outlined above.

implications of becoming expert campus consultants

Although consultation is just one method of intervention whose importance should not be overstressed, it is a significant method, with many potential implications for the profession. Consultation characterized by excellence can enhance our functioning in three major ways.

Enhancement of Individual Professional Identity. A student services professional who becomes expert in using the consultation process to convey expertise in a specific knowledge or skill area will also acquire a sharpened self-concept and a more substantial professional identity. The ability to identify and convey a professional repertoire is critical to a feeling of pride in what one accomplishes. The very activity of defining oneself as a consultant forces the consultant into determining what skills and knowledge she or he really has; there is a difference between talking about and actually demonstrating or teaching a skill or knowledge area. In this way consultation works to force us into an acknowledgment of what we can — and cannot — do.

Higher Credibility of Student Services. Excellence in consultation will elicit respect from the rest of the academic community for that particular skill; it will also generalize to enhance credibility of other programs and activities in the student services area. In fact, counsel, advice, and consultation have always been expected from us by the academic community. There is an expectation that we will know about students and their characteristics. This expectation has been fulfilled too inconsistently in the past. With a new commitment to the foundation of student-environment interaction, along with intervention tools such as consultation, student services stands on the threshold of a new era of respect and credibility with our academic colleagues.

Clarification and Integration of the Role of Student Services. The student services profession has existed for years under the *in loco parentis* rationale, functioning as an inadequately defined applied specialty. This has led to the weaknesses in content, research, and training mentioned earlier.

Becoming competent consultants helps clarify our professional identity in several ways: it is a specific and powerful skill, a concrete and essential tool in our professional armamentarium. Also, training in the art and science of consultation would enhance training curricula in student personnel, providing graduates with one more identifiable area of expertise. Secondly, there has been little work in applying the rather extensive body of theoretical writing about consultation to higher education. This allows the student services profession to focus on developing a research base unique to its function which will in turn contribute to the stature of the profession. Third, the division of student services that can list consultation among its intervention strategies is likely to be in touch with its ability to influence and shape the educational environment. This sense of power is a desirable replacement for the feelings of professional impotence that too often characterize student services professionals. In an ideal setting, the various components of a student services division would have a set of shared goals, techniques, and conceptual frameworks. This a desirable alternative to the frequent situation of a conglomerate of separate agencies tied together only by administrative convenience. Consultation has potential for contributing to the achievement of common goals because of its ability to be used by student services professionals with a wide variety of backgrounds and functions; it is a truly sharable technique. Finally, there is no designated agency or group in higher education identified as the one to continuously assess and monitor the all-important interaction between students and their environment. This function is of critical importance to the mission of higher education, and student services at present has the most potential to fill the void. Consultation is the tool which can allow us to move into this new and integrative role. Added to other emerging concepts and skills, it will play a vital role in the profession's assuming its rightful place as a central influence in the educational and administrative mission of colleges and universities.

reference

Morrill, W. H., Oetting, E. R., and Hurst, J. C. "Dimensions of Counselor Functioning." *Personnel and Guidance Journal*, 1974, *52*, 354–359.

James C. Hurst is dean of students, assistant vice president for student affairs, and associate professor of counseling psychology at the University of Texas at Austin. He is particularly interested in delivery systems and programming for human development, and is one of the authors of the award-winning article "Dimensions of Counselor Functioning" which appeared in the February 1974 issue of the Personnel and Guidance Journal. *Dr. Hurst views consultation as one of the most important strategies available to human development specialists for broad-scale intervention.*

Further sources for those interested in pursuing the topic of campus consultation are provided in this chapter.

wrap-up with annotated references

m. kathryn hamilton
charles j. meade

In some ideal world, at the end of an issue such as this we might be able to say: there you have it; that is the definitive story. The somewhat frustrating— and equally exciting—truth is, however, that campus consultation activities are far from clearly defined. The story is unfinished. Contributors to this issue reflect the varying opinions of student services staff in how broadly they define the goals of consultation/mediated services. There are, however, a number of major themes which appear throughout the chapters.

First, there is a growing awareness that student services professionals must think in terms of the whole university system—or beyond—when creating goals and evaluating their work. Whether the goal is to affect the entire community or to confine our activities within a more traditionally defined sphere—it is no longer possible, and perhaps not ethical, to be naive about the fact that our efforts affect parts of the system in addition to the most direct recipients. Understanding the ripple effect is necessary; taking positive advantage of it is a worthwhile challenge. Defining our consultation activities, clarifying their goals, and using existing models are all necessary steps.

The complexities of consulting in a multilevel system, where staff at the same level may be consulting with each other in a quasi-expert context, are evident. This puts campus consultants in particular binds. To best serve our campuses, we need at times to serve each other. Open discussion about the difficulties in such multiple relationships and (again) thinking always in terms of our shared goals will help in minimizing our binds.

Committing ourselves to more awareness of our consultative efforts and to improving them demands both high quality evaluation and accountability. The need for both is recognized by all authors.

A theme which is present in all chapters, though more implicit in some, is the idea that in many ways campus consultation is a political activity. If our aim is to affect the environment to promote student development, then we must acknowledge and deal with political and power issues. All social change is political, and working with campus environments will require us to be sensitive, dynamic, and—this is critical—accepting of conflict.

Little has been written about the developmental stages of campus agencies or divisions, or about the life cycles of university systems. Making ourselves competent consultants necessitates our being increasingly able to predict future events, and to see and analyze the ones we did not predict. If we are to consult to our campuses, the demands are great. We must have broad goals without being unrealistic or grandiose; we must be able to see the whole picture without losing our specific direction; we must have a plan without being rigid; we must have values without being messianic; and we must be willing to take leadership without being elitist. To achieve all that, we must be able to work within the real and immediate present, while never forgetting to move toward a future we can help create.

If we did not see the task as important, this issue would not have been possible; if we did not see the problems as complex, this issue would not have been necessary; and if we did not see the enterprise as exciting, this issue would not have been as challenging as it has been.

additional sources of information

Providing useful resources for campus consultants is a difficult task. The literature on consultation is vast; materials specifically addressing consultation on campus are rare. Because of our belief that the consultant can best proceed by developing a useful conceptual framework for his/her activities— and because of the lack of integrated writing about campus consultation— most of the following are theoretical or broad treatments which we think will offer a solid grounding in key concepts and knowledge areas. Though specific applications or programs rarely appear in the list below, most authors do use valuable and clear applied examples in their discussions which should be of use to consultants.

Consultation Theory, Practice, and Evaluation

Atkisson, C. C., and others. *Evaluation of Human Service Programs.* New York: Academic Press, 1978.

Designed for those who administer and evaluate social service programs of any kind, this is one of the best and broadest handbooks of its kind; a wealth of information in a clearly written style.

Bennis, W. G., and others (Eds.). *The Planning of Change.* New York: Holt, Rinehart and Winston, 1976.

Focusing on the planful application of knowledge in human affairs in order to create action plans and change, this collection of articles provides the reader with a comprehensive look at systems, environments, and the nature of change; as such, it is invaluable for those consultants who view themselves as change agents and systems thinkers.

Blake, R. R., and Mouton, J. S. *Consultation.* Reading, Mass.: Addison-Wesley, 1976.

These well-known consultants have attempted to articulate a systematic, integrated theory of consultation, and they identify central patterns, then organize them in a three-dimensional model.

Caplan, G. *The Theory and Practice of Mental Health Consultation.* New York: Basic Books, 1970.

Appropriate for all campus consultants, this book includes theoretically based consultation guidelines, with case examples, illustrating a respectful, nonintrusive style.

Kurpius, D. J. (Ed.). "Consultation I . . . definition — models — programs." *Personnel and Guidance Journal,* 1978, *56* (6), whole issue.

Kurpius, D. J. (Ed.). "Consultation II . . . dimensions — training — bibliography." *Personnel and Guidance Journal,* 1978, *56* (7), whole issue.

A two-volume special issue, this is an attempt to elucidate major theories, issues, and knowledge about consultation; it includes specific examples and programs as well as theory. A large bibliography makes it an invaluable resource. Of special note:

Westbrook, F. D., and others. "University Campus Consultation Through the Formation of Collaborative Dyads." *Personnel and Guidance Journal.* 1978, *56* (6), 359-363.

These authors report on a model program for campus consultation and discuss in a lively, direct manner organizational issues that arise when student services colleagues consult with one another.

Schein, E. H. *Process Consultation.* Reading, Mass.: Addison-Wesley, 1969.

Focuses on the process (non-content) aspects of the consultative relationship; especially useful for consultants in ongoing relationships with consultees who must listen to the music as well as the words.

Systems

Bertalanffy, L. *General System Theory.* New York: George Braziller, 1968.

The seminal book on systems theory, it offers a coherent, pragmatic perspective for thinking about human systems, and, by extension, service to those systems.

Cowen, E. "Social and Community Interventions." *Annual Review of Psychology*, 1973, *24*, 423–472.

Though focused on community interventions to affect mental health and emotional functioning, this review touches on several topics of critical interest to student services staff, such as environmental engineering and the use of consultation to enhance environments.

Laszlo, E. (Ed.). *The Relevance of General Systems Theory*. New York: George Braziller, 1972.

A collection of essays on the diverse applications of general systems theory, multidisciplinary, but especially focused on social sciences and services.

*M. Kathryn Hamilton is senior psychologist at the
University Counseling Center and assistant professor of
psychology at Colorado State University.*

*Charles J. Meade is assistant professor of
counseling psychology and coordinator of consultation in the
University Counseling Service at the University of Iowa.*

index

New Directions Quarterly Sourcebooks

New Directions for Student Services is one of several distinct series of quarterly sourcebooks published by Jossey-Bass. The sourcebooks in each series are designed to serve both as *convenient compendiums* of the latest knowledge and practical experience on their topics and as *long-life reference tools.*

One-year, four-sourcebook subscriptions for each series cost $15 for individuals (when paid by personal check) and $25 for institutions, libraries, and agencies. Current 1979 sourcebooks are available by subscription only (however, multiple copies—five or more—are available for workshops or classroom use at $5.95 per copy). Single copies of earlier sourcebooks are available at $5.95 each.

A complete listing is given below of current and past sourcebooks in the *New Directions for Student Services* series. The titles and editors-in-chief of the other series are also listed. To subscribe, or to receive further information, write: New Directions Subscriptions, Jossey-Bass Inc., Publishers, 433 California Street, San Francisco, California 94104.

New Directions for Student Services
Ursula Delworth and Gary R. Hanson, Editors-in-Chief
1978: 1. *Evaluating Program Effectiveness,* Gary R. Hanson
       2. *Training Competent Staff,* Ursula Delworth
       3. *Reducing the Dropout Rate,* Lee Noel
       4. *Applying New Developmental Findings,* Lee Knefelkamp, Carole Widick, Clyde A. Parker

New Directions for Child Development
William Damon, Editor-in-Chief

New Directions for Community Colleges
Arthur M. Cohen, Editor-in-Chief
Florence B. Brawer, Associate Editor

New Directions for Continuing Education
Alan B. Knox, Editor-in-Chief

New Directions for Education and Work
Lewis C. Solmon, Editor-in-Chief

New Directions for Experiential Learning
Morris T. Keeton and Pamela J. Tate, Editors-in-Chief

New Directions for Higher Education
JB Lon Hefferlin, Editor-in-Chief

New Directions for Institutional Advancement
A. Westley Rowland, Editor-in-Chief

New Directions for Institutional Research
Marvin W. Peterson, Editor-in-Chief

New Directions for Mental Health Services
H. Richard Lamb, Editor-in-Chief

New Directions for Program Evaluation
Scarvia B. Anderson, Editor-in-Chief